LIVING IN THE FLOW: PRACTICING VIBRATIONAL ALIGNMENT

RUTH CHERRY, PhD

BALBOA.
PRESS
A DIVISION OF HAY HOUSE

Copyright © 2015 Ruth Cherry.

All rights reserved. No part of this book may be used or reproduced by
any means, graphic, electronic, or mechanical, including photocopying,
recording, taping or by any information storage retrieval system
without the written permission of the author except in the case of
brief quotations embodied in critical articles and reviews.

Balboa Press books may be ordered through booksellers or by contacting:

Balboa Press
A Division of Hay House
1663 Liberty Drive
Bloomington, IN 47403
www.balboapress.com
1 (877) 407-4847

Because of the dynamic nature of the Internet, any web addresses or
links contained in this book may have changed since publication and
may no longer be valid. The views expressed in this work are solely those
of the author and do not necessarily reflect the views of the publisher,
and the publisher hereby disclaims any responsibility for them.

The author of this book does not dispense medical advice or prescribe the use
of any technique as a form of treatment for physical, emotional, or medical
problems without the advice of a physician, either directly or indirectly. The
intent of the author is only to offer information of a general nature to help
you in your quest for emotional and spiritual well-being. In the event you use
any of the information in this book for yourself, which is your constitutional
right, the author and the publisher assume no responsibility for your actions.

Any people depicted in stock imagery provided by Thinkstock are models,
and such images are being used for illustrative purposes only.
Certain stock imagery © Thinkstock.

Print information available on the last page.

ISBN: 978-1-5043-2893-7 (sc)
ISBN: 978-1-5043-2894-4 (e)

Balboa Press rev. date: 11/21/2016

I dedicate this book to Rev. Leona Evans and Unity of San Luis Obispo, California. I appreciate your wisdom, guidance, and support.

CONTENTS

FOREWORD

Ruth Cherry gives new meaning to the often heard phrase "Walking the Talk."

From a viral infection in her 20s to a recent diagnosis of Multiple Sclerosis, Ruth has had tremendous difficulty with the physical act of walking. But her difficulties were not just physical. Ruth suffered deep emotional wounds from a lifetime of self-loathing, feelings of inadequacy and rejection, and an abusive subpersonality – someone she calls the Controller.

In the first part of this book, Ruth shares her very personal story via her intimate journal entries. We are given a front row seat to witness how she transformed not only her physical abilities but her overall life, and probably even more importantly, her emotional and spiritual well-being. It's been a long journey. With raw and riveting honesty, she shares the deep inner work that it took – being willing to tell the truth, facing her relentless critical self-talk and sense of hopelessness, choosing to unconditionally love and accept herself and others – just to name a few. She takes us along with her as she learns how to practice the divine laws of true healing, what Ruth calls "Living in the Flow."

I have a deep sense of awe and amazement at her ability to share as she has in this book. It's not her nature to be so self-disclosing.

Being willing to share her most private thoughts and personal information is a testimony to the healing that has happened for her. She generously uses this deeply personal information as an introduction and an invitation for us all to do the same inner work.

In the second part of the book, Ruth begins to share her wisdom on "Practicing Vibrational Alignment." There is something about her writing that helps me to breathe. As I go through these chapters, I let go, I release, and I experience. This is the mark of a true teacher. Ruth has an ability to make these practices real and even easy. She creates the space for us to experience what she is explaining. When I read the piece on gratitude, I could feel gratitude seeping into my consciousness. When she tells us over and over again, it's a matter of allowing, I find myself silently saying YES.

In this second part of the book Ruth shares her professional knowledge of the psychology of living a spiritual life. She helps us to understand operating from our Child vs. our Adult subpersonalities. She highlights the tasks of integrating the lightness and the darkness in our lives. She explains the value of embracing our vulnerability. She gently leads us to the power of taking responsibility for our own healing and happiness.

I also love her focus on mid-life psychology. There is a shift in mid-life. We all know it. We move from the earlier concerns and tasks of identity and achievement into the call for our creativity and our spirituality to be expressed. She invites us to be the Hero of our own lives and shows us how to get there through meditation.

I believe Ruth's greatest gift is her ability to teach the practice of meditation. I have been a regular member of her daily meditation group for over a year. And it has been a life-changing experience. In this book she is able to lay out the process and the requirements for a deep meditation practice that will yield for us what we are seeking – the ability to be present, the willingness to be open, the belief in the possibility of a Controller-free life. She carefully outlines a path to our inner worlds, inner quiet, and the peace we all seek.

Finally, we are shown how meditation opens the door to Spirituality. We see how, when we relax into the oneness that arises from pure consciousness, we come into presence, beingness, grace - the world of Source. She provides exercises and scripts as well as a very comprehensive explanation as to why we do what we do in meditation. It both demystifies it and retains its mystical, magical essence.

In the final section, Ruth does an in-depth job of describing the spiritual qualities we are all seeking. This is a comprehensive section that covers almost everything – from finding our true selves, to deep forgiveness and what that means, to the beauty of grace, and the ultimate power of opening to Source.

I've often felt incomplete in my understanding of what Source is and how it feels in our everyday lives. Ruth talks about Source in a way that covers all of the benefits and all the difficulties with living in alignment with Source Consciousness. She helps us to see how being connected to Source is the ultimate healer. This is our true power. This is what allows us to be the peacemakers we all need to be in this world. It's not just about our healing. We do this for everyone and everything. When you finish reading this book, you will feel this in the core of your being. You will feel lifted up and connected and ready to say YES to life.

Meister Eckhart says that the greatest prayer is always to simply say Thank You.

Thank You, Ruth, for your heart, your work, and your calling. Anyone who picks up this book and reads it will be moved further on their path. And you, dear Ruth, keep on walking!

Kathy Murphy, Ph.D.
Author, **Your Possible Life – How to Build the Life of Your Dreams**
www.KathyMurphy.com

INTRODUCTION

The diagnosis of Multiple Sclerosis was bestowed upon me at the first of the year. I was told by well-meaning friends that it was not such a terrible pronouncement. Everyone knew someone who was performing brilliantly with an MS label. However, having that stamp applied to me was horrifying. It took me three months to accept the news.

The medical personnel I encountered along the way were more than competent, highly efficient, and caring. They had seen MS patients deteriorate and knew what to expect. They told me to remove my throw rugs, to use a cane, and to rest. No one said, "And this will happen to you, also," but the expectation was clear. I felt defeated.

At the urging of two close friends I started journal writing. I have journalled extensively over my professional career as a psychologist and an author. All of my books originated with a journal entry. I've worked through feelings, cleared my thoughts, and anchored myself with journal writing. It has given me a way to cope with uncomfortable life events. This diagnosis presented the most intimidating challenge I've faced.

Journal writing invites the unconscious to come forth. I create a space by sitting at my computer, focusing my attention, and opening to receive words or images or feelings. I have learned to respect the wisdom of my unconscious. I received my doctorate in 1976 and have practiced individual psychotherapy since then. I watch as healing emerges from the confusion or anger or pain that clients bring. Certainly, I have witnessed this unconscious healing process in myself, also. When I wait for my unconscious to lead me, I observe my thoughts and feelings and record what I notice in my journal. I don't introduce an intellectual component; I just pay attention. And then I write what I observe. Always I am surprised by the unfolding. And delighted. Our inner worlds hold such depth and intricacy and mystery. They lead us to a healing our minds can't predict.

So, over this background of trust for my inner world direction, I introduce the diagnosis of MS with my reactions of frustration, sadness, fear, confusion, surprise, and, eventually, determination. Finally, I welcomed this diagnosis as an opportunity.

I wrote often, I meditated, and I used my background as a psychologist to structure my observations. I don't encourage dwelling in the past, but as the unconscious heals it resolves old wounds and mistaken beliefs. I noticed that, allowed it, and watched it pass. My appreciation for my psychodynamics made sense of my experience.

I, also, used my knowledge of the Enneagram, a tool for psychological and spiritual healing and transformation. This test points out specifically and clearly the blocks, challenges, dynamics, and strengths for each of us. This is the done in the context of "types." We each fall into one of nine types with its own motivations and insights and blind spots. When we learn our type, we recognize the distortions in our thinking and perceptions and maintain a more objective stance in regards to our inner world. Each type experiences healing and transformation by meditating.

Meditation invites a powerful healing intervention from an unknown Source. When we meditate we allow the unconscious to guide us in a slightly altered state. In journal writing the conscious mind cooperates with the unconscious by recording the words, images, feelings, and thoughts. When we meditate we ask the conscious mind to wait outside the door and we create a space for the unconscious to move. We observe, we allow, and, always, we stay present. Daily meditation brings healing shifts into our lives all through the week, not only while we sit. We invite the Universe to partner with us and the Universe always says, Yes.

Working with the unconscious on both a personal and a transpersonal level has led to an evolution of my thinking about spirituality. Reality is greater than we can understand. We participate in the whole from our individual perspective. The Abraham/Hicks material has lent an immensely helpful structure to my understanding. Thoughts create reality. This is good news since we can change our thoughts at will. But it is not always simple or easy. Unconscious psychodynamics intervene. Our commitment to meditation empowers our self-awareness by showing us those psychodynamics. We don't have to understand what happens in meditation; the Universe does its work without our input. We just need to get in the chair and meditate.

In Part One, I share my journal writing for seven months. I invite you to walk with me as I experience and learn. In Part Two I offer you support in your journey. The first section focuses on good mental health practices from a psychological viewpoint. The second section offers guidance about committing to your meditation practice. The third section presents some thoughts about self-affirming spiritual practices. I offer you these thoughts to apply to your own experience.

These pages recount the most powerful days of my life. I wish you power and wisdom and clarity in your journey.

PART ONE

JOURNAL WRITING

April 30

This week I start a new drug. The fact that it is new, just an addition to an ever-lengthening list of drugs, surprises me just a little. I have believed that with good judgment, adequate exercise, healthy eating habits, and decent sleep (when I can find it), I could maintain a good quality of health. I not only wanted to do it all myself, I thought I must. I didn't expect help.

When I was 20, 18 months into a miserable marriage and just completing college in Chicago, I was brought down by a virus I contracted in a Lake Michigan winter wind. I had lived two years in South Bend, Ind., for my initial college experience. The first Oct. I was there in 1967, I was entranced by the snowfall. In Oklahoma we didn't see much snow and never saw it for very long. Here the flakes bombarded the campus, the cars, the people and accumulated on the ground, the trees, and the buildings. For weeks and months. In May it was still snowing but I was no longer delighted.

After two years in South Bend I transferred to the University of Illinois in Chicago. The snow was still plentiful but added to it were the gusts off the lake. I was colder than I had ever been and for longer. In December, 1970, when I finished the required coursework to earn a BS, I had another cold. When the cold had resolved in Jan. I noticed some weakness in my right leg which grew worse. I was at home in Tulsa, visiting my parents for Christmas, but when it came time to return to Chicago, I, instead, entered the hospital. Where I remained for 44 days.

I slept 22 hours a day without meds. I had no pain but also very little feeling and less control of any muscles. My vision doubled at a short distance, I couldn't hold a spoon, and standing was out of the question.

When I left the hospital I had received the diagnosis of transverse myelitis. According to the doctors, a virus from the cold had entered my spinal fluid and damaged nerves. My right leg and left arm were most affected. The doctors said to swim and to expect that I would age faster than usual. They didn't limit my expectations for my healing but also didn't offer any long term therapies.

The result was that I believed my healing was up to me. I was 21 and still fairly steeped in denial so I really didn't see much of a problem. I didn't walk for four months but gradually my strength returned. I didn't doubt that I would recover so I was completely optimistic.

I entered graduate school that fall at the University of Oklahoma in Norman and enjoyed a fairly normal graduate experience — long hours in the library, weekend drinking, limited sleep, and lots of walking. My body grew stronger.

The next years took me to southern Ohio for my first job in a psychiatric hospital and then to southern California for a doctorate. Starting in Ohio and continuing in California, I swam as the doctors had recommended. I had been as athletic as any girl in a girls' school in Oklahoma was — not very. Summers in Oklahoma kept everyone inside from 9-6. Evenings were lovely, catching fireflies and stringing dandelions. But outside activity was limited.

In California, however, I was amazed and delighted by the gentle days and nights. In the winters it rained. I thought I was in paradise. San Diego in the 1970s was an overgrown town with friendly folks and multifarious opportunities to explore interests of every ilk. I jogged, painted watercolors, attended artist's receptions, wrote and attended author's receptions, drank wine on the beach, made a skydiving jump, climbed the vertical trail by Torrey Pines golf course to the beach. Additionally, I maintained a private practice doing psychotherapy, kept my own books under the tutelage from my CPA father, and bought a condominium. Life was great.

I pursued my interest in meditation. The last quarter in graduate school I learned to meditate, perhaps the most helpful course I took. But life was busy in my 20s with activities and in my 30s with work. By 40 and thereafter, unpaid inner world bills had come due. It was time to delve deeply into my shadowy undercurrents.

The psychological framework provided by my studies and my work helped me appreciate the order and the beauty and the precision of my own psychodynamics. Meditation gave me a construct for holding the craziness and pain and overwhelm. I had developed a strong Controller, the part of me who insisted that I function rationally in the world. But my feeling side had been neglected. Now it demanded attention and in meditation found it.

My 40s proved to be less about work and more about integrating my unconscious dynamics. Meanwhile, I swam four days a week and went to the gym to lift weights and use the cardio machines three days. Physically, I didn't grow stronger as I had until 40, but I maintained my physical competence.

My meditations deepened my self-awareness, as though an inner teacher showed me flip cards and said, "Look at this and this and this." Details from every age appeared, I looked at them, experienced my feelings, and watched them pass. I respected the wisdom in my meditations which clearly wasn't related to my intellect. I lived more spontaneously.

Menopause at 55 issued in startling and devastating physical changes. I had visited China, contracted a cold, taken Cipro and returned to the US. No big concern. I didn't have another period and "felt" a pool dry up inside me. Each day I walked with more difficulty.

The nerve damage symptoms from 1971 returned incrementally. I was left in pain, without much muscle control, and unable to think clearly. After consulting three doctors, I established a hormone replacement regimen which helped immensely but not completely. I still couldn't walk evenly.

It has been nine years since then and I've found a wonderful doctor who measured and replaced amino acids. I swim a mile daily and I feel great. But walking is still a challenge. A physical therapist has given me some pertinent exercises which I practice religiously. But I've also noticed that my healing is more than just physical. A spiritual component has developed from my many hours meditating which guides me. I've learned to expect support from non-physical reality and to look for it. And it always comes. Now I value my partnership with non-physical reality and rely on it. I've learned that blending the physical and non-physical parts of me defines true healing.

May 4

I had anticipated the new medication hopefully because I was told it would yield immediate benefits to my walking with no side effects. Quite the opposite was true. Within two hours of taking the first pill dizziness prevented me from standing. Now almost 24 hours later I still don't feel myself. I'm glad I tried it since I want to explore every option the doctors provide. They seem to resist death but be OK with medication destroying my quality of life. What's the sense in that?

Now I am more sure that my healing is up to me. This morning I am speaking at Unity while the minister is out of town. My topic is vibrating at the frequency of Source. We are all physical and non-physical beings and we always, always emanate a vibration. What are we emanating?

If we know as Source knows, we create a reality vibrationally aligned with Source. If we doubt or think or believe, we separate ourselves from Source. True healing is practicing that aligned vibration all the time. I don't think the doctors practice that alignment. They offer a cure (or partial cure) from their intellects. They trust their minds more than their Source energy centers. They believe, they don't trust their experience. Bless them. They do the best they can but they can't offer me what I need to heal. I am, this morning, more than I have ever been, sure that my healing is up to my vibrational practice.

At church I will lead the congregation in imagining their perfect healing, in whatever terms that takes. And I will practice this, also. For ten minutes a day I will know myself healing. I will visualize myself healed, aligned with Source. No thinking, no belief, no action. Simply knowing and allowing.

Allowing the Universe to work in my life is trusting Source completely, jumping off the edge, acknowledging that I haven't a parachute, and watching to see what happens. Besides having no alternative at this point, I want to live this way. I want to embrace passion and trust and total surrender. I want to say, "Your will be done." I'm clear that I can do no more under my own steam. All the pushing and exercising and discipline hasn't carried me the last miles of my healing. I am glad I practice good habits but I need more. And Source is my only hope at this point.

And not such a puny hope, either. The power that creates worlds is available to me and to each of us. All we need say is, "I'm available." And then practice vibrational alignment with the Universe.

I can do that. I want to do that. I choose to be a vibrational match to my own healing. I choose to focus on the solution, not on the problem. I choose to align with the Universe, not with my intellect or my hard work or with the doctors' acceptance of limitation. I have hope and knowing and trust.

May 6

I discussed my difficulty with the drug with my friend, Amber. A decades long meditator, she immediately responded, "Trust your intuition." Today on the treadmill at the gym walking 1.4 miles an hour, focusing on rolling my foot as the physical therapist had instructed, a thought came to ingest only a few grains from the capsule, not the whole capsule.

I do notice today that I'm not walking as well as I did the last two. Maybe the drug did some good. I will trust my intuition and experiment with the drug and with my exercise. And await further intuitive marching instructions.

I am a vibrational being in this vibrational Universe. I practice aligning my vibration with Source and devote time specifically for that every day. That's the most I need do. And listen. And know that my good comes to me now.

May 7

I swallowed a few grains of the drug last night and thought/hoped I felt a slight tingling in my legs as though they were waking up. This morning I feel my right leg more connected to the ground and I'm able to tuck my hips under. I also walk a teeny bit better. These were the first presenting symptoms nine years ago when I lost so much. Thus, I suspect the drug is beneficial but I must experiment to find the appropriate dose. Tonight I'll ingest a bit more.

This feels like an answer to my prayers and a big answer at that. I recognize that I've felt more guided since I started practicing the Abraham/Hicks material less than a year ago. I learned that I must forgive and release, I must stay in the present and appreciate, and that spiritual forces notice me every second. Doing these practices seems to remove a block which allows me to receive.

May 17

Swimming laps this morning, I think about my excitement/hope about healing and my weariness. In addition to swimming a mile, I've added floor exercises, walking on the treadmill, and a few machines at the gym. My Controller is ready to jump into action and to direct my progress. My fatigue tells me that needs to stop.

My Controller is the part of me that thinks, plans, acts. She strove and succeeded in my early life. It was a thrill to push hard and to meet the next goal. When the doctor prescribed the medicine, the Controller thought it was her cue to rev up. So I pushed as hard as I could, exercised more than I had for years, and knew I was returning to my younger self.

But no. Instead, I am exhausted. I'm developing a weakness in my right shoulder which I push through when I swim but I respect with the weights.

My frustration that I looked at when swimming this morning was realizing that my Controller was active but unsuccessful. How much have I (unconsciously) allowed this part of me to direct my thinking all my life? Controllers in other folks have always annoyed me, but now I'm seeing how large and pervasive my own Controller is. And it's not working.

After I swam I meditated with my friend, Vicki. The weekly meditation groups have been suspended due to the church's move and I've missed them. In our meditation this morning I realized that my Controller is not the part of me that will carry me to healing. In fact, if she is very involved not much good will follow. My guidance is to trust and to allow inspiration to guide me, not to power through based on my strong will or my intellect's goals. I need to allow Source to pull me to healing. And to trust the process.

I need to go to the gym when I'm inspired to do so, not because it's the next item on my To Do list. I learned to trust my inspiration when I was writing books and articles. It's a lovely cooperative partnership with the Universe. I listen, I wait to receive, and I respond. It worked well for me writing five books. It was fun, otherworldly, and not of my mind's creation.

Why does trusting that same process now for my physical healing scare me? Am I afraid that if I don't control the process it won't unfold beneficially? I see what happens when my Controller is active and it's not good. As my meditation showed me, I need to trust and to allow and to know that my healing is proceeding. I need to acknowledge that other forces are at work and to let them pull me. I've done it before. In fact, I do it every day as part of my spiritual practice.

And here the rubber meets the road, so to speak. This is the bottom line, the most important issue in my life, the goal I want more than anything — to walk well again. And I'm shown I can't work on it. I can't "try." I can only trust.

We use our strengths in the first part of our lives to achieve success. Now well into my second half of life I am shown I must embrace the vulnerability that so annoyed me in the first half of life. Then it threatened to derail my success. Now it is the only access to the path to my dreams. That's how we partner with Source, through our vulnerability. So, now that is the part of me I must attend to and love.

For me that means allowing much "time under the bridge." Allowing and appreciating instead of scheming and efforting. Noticing what comes instead of orchestrating the next move.

Dare I trust Source in this, the most important experiment of my life? Yes, I'm ready to trust and to surrender. I'm overjoyed about the opportunity to practice. Meditation turns on the light for me so I can see what's happening in my head and in my heart. And then I choose stillness and I watch.

June 4

Today it occurs to me that I can give in. Not give up, but give in to the well-being that surrounds and envelops me. That endless stream that keeps flowing until my mind with its incessant thoughts chokes it. Why not choose to be "at the bottom of the barrel" where the healing shift occurs. That's where I say, "I cannot do this with my own will; I surrender." I don't give up but I shift my orientation and give it to Source.

And I wait and I practice receiving and I look for instances of my good coming. The second Source hears my desire, Source sees me with that desire fulfilled. I choose to see myself that way, to know that my healing is true now regardless of the "evidence," and to celebrate my oneness with Source by living joyfully. I choose to see my desires fulfilled. I choose to live joyfully regardless of my circumstances. I choose to know rather than to hope or to believe or to ask.

I know that reality starts inside with my knowing the truth of my healing. I will see it when I know it. First, I practice vibrating at the frequency of Source. As I am one with Source, I know what Source knows. And Source already knows that I am healed. I simply allow that healing.

Big things are the same as small things to Source. I always get the parking places I need. I always find what's lost. I am guided to meet the folks I need to know. Doors I don't see open. I see Source working every day in my life so I know healing is mine. And knowing that, I go about my life and look for gifts.

June 14

Tomorrow I again will speak at church while the minister is away. I will lead with Jung's story about the African village suffering terribly from an extended drought. A shaman entered the village and walked into the center where a tent awaited him. After three days, rain poured. When asked what he "did," he replied that he had picked up so much imbalance walking through the village, he knew he must restore his own inner balance before the environment would reflect balance.

Preparing this talk, I have consciously noticed my own vibrational practice. I tried an experiment. I affirmed that a tiny spot on my cheek would disappear. Daily I said, "The spot on my cheek — thanks for removing it." Yesterday a second spot appeared!

I didn't realize that I was focusing on the problem instead of the solution. Whatever I focus on increases. This experiment delights me because I can see the Universe responding immediately and precisely to me. I understand how I need to re-focus. I need to see my cheek healthy and even. I need to see my walking healthy and comfortable.

I need to know perfect health for myself, to really know it in my heart. Intellectual affirmations prove irrelevant and, worse than that, they lead me away from the Source of my power.

I'm trusting and knowing that Source will heal my completely. Rationally, this is nonsense but rationality has nothing to do with healing. I know how to align my vibrations with Source. I know how to practice vibrational integrity. I totally trust my oneness. That's all I need.

I'm going to have so much fun noticing the little signs of my healing. It's no longer a question of "if" but "how" and "when" and I'm not impatient. My goodness comes to me and I receive it joyfully.

June 17

After my talk at church on Sunday, I challenged the congregation to treat themselves the way Source treats them for one second — to unconditionally accept and love themselves. To be 100% on their own side. To adore themselves. For one second.

The talk went well enough but I came home and was overwhelmed with old feelings of hate from my abusive Inner Critic. No words, just contempt. Not for anything I had done or said just for me being me and allowing myself to be known.

Two days later, after spending much time in meditation and contemplation, I realize that asking for complete physical healing has opened me to healing at a deeper level. I have known about and felt the self-loathing for decades but I see now that healing my body requires that I love myself as Source loves me. By asking for healing I have allowed the light to shine in the shadowy corners where the anger still lives. I didn't know it was there but I can feel the familiar ache. Now I know it can be healed.

Physical healing isn't just physical or even primarily physical. I first became ill when I was married at 19, a horrible relationship. I sought love because I thought I was unlovable. Of course, the marriage didn't work but that was the setting when I became ill with nerve damage impairing my walking.

Now I need to find and experience that healing inside me and to allow it to heal me. How can I be whole physically if I'm not healed emotionally or spiritually? Now I can love myself, the basis for my healing.

June 20

Leona Evans, the minister at Unity, came to lunch this week, a first for us. I felt scared and a little desperate one day last week when I invited her. I have often thought that one reason I am in this area is to learn from her. She is able to see me and to "get" me in a way no one else does.

When she asks me how I am, I tell her everything. Immediately, she is totally present and attentive. She also has chronic conditions and lives with pain. (I am so grateful I don't have pain.) Leona is open with her vulnerability but is not overwhelmed by it. I told her I am committed to doing my own healing regardless of the diagnosis and the medical professionals' expectations. She encourages me in that as well as acknowledging the value of western medicine. She names several folks who have healed themselves and are doing beautifully, very publicly.

When she mentions the service last Sunday (when I substituted for her) I tell her about my Critic's reaction and my two day depression. In her book, **Spirituality and Self-Esteem**, she offers a process to know and work with the Critic. Her Critic she named Aunt Rose. By naming the figure she gives it boundaries and anchors it in one place. I chose Mary to name my Critic.

The first part of my life was about control and Mary was dominant. I tried pleasing, biting my tongue, fitting into the mold presented to me. The consequences were devastating to my sense of myself. I didn't integrate my anger or learn to trust it and use it. Assertion was just a concept. I accepted chronic depression, the natural result of being hated by this huge Critic.

The second part of my life is about moving beyond the Critic. The three step process Leona teaches is O D E — Observing the Critic, practicing Discernment, and Embracing the Critic. In my meditations I am good at assuming a passive Observer stance. But this last time I just watched the out-of-control, condemning Critic for two days. Nothing resolved. The next step is realizing that this Critic is immature, irresponsible, and very afraid. She doesn't want me to be hurt in the world so she demands that I hide. That's the best strategy she can devise.

I have felt her abuse in her relentless criticism of me since childhood. Sometimes I have heard her words from another's mouth but now I can see that it's all me. I may unconsciously project this hateful figure but I'm very clear it originates inside. And I need to take the next step and take back the power I have given her. She is no one special. She isn't as mature as an eight year-old. I need to parent her. She is mine to raise. She obviously needs my attention so I stay in my Adult and provide the guidance she needs. Passivity in the face of her immature abuse doesn't address the imbalance. So, I move into my powerful Adult and rise above the situation and redirect her ire.

In "real" life this is something I haven't done well. I have allowed myself to be victimized in groups and in one-to-one situations. These relationships reflected the abusive relationship inside. All the time I was longing for love and acceptance. Sometimes I settled for approval which never quite satisfied. Frequently, I felt misunderstood, unseen, and not wanted. A sad and sometimes miserable way to go through life.

Could my need for self-acceptance and love somehow be intertwined with my debilitating physical symptoms?

The second part of my life is about moving beyond the Critic, about owning my power, and about moving out of Victim and into my Wise Adult.

It's becoming clearer to me that my Controller cannot choreograph my healing intellectually. (She thinks and plans and organizes.) Going to the gym, doing more and more and more isn't working. After so many days of swimming a mile in the morning and walking a mile on the treadmill in the afternoon, I feel weaker. So I've stopped most of the walking for the last two weeks and rested more.

I can see how allowing is my only hope. Of course, that would be true. To heal I need to do the opposite of what I was doing when the situation arose. I also need to give my healing to Source, not to try and force it through my Controller. I need to give Source all the credit and to allow Source to guide me.

Leona left me with this affirmation: Mighty currents of God's healing love flow through me now making me whole and free.

June 21

Yesterday the home health care nurse, Nancy, came to my home to show me how to do the injections which will slow the progression of the disease. When we spoke on the phone, I was resistant. I had heard that I would be sick for a day a week and I don't want to invite more disability. She heard my hesitation and came the next day so as not to give me time to think.

We practiced and practiced. As my anxiety increased so did my giggling. When it was time for me to plunge the syringe into my leg I burst into tears. That seems so wrong. She told me to breathe and kept perfect eye contact. I did it and it was nothing. No pain, no feeling at all really, and over quickly. The first week is 1/4 dose, increasing each of the next three weeks until we reach the full dose which maintains for the rest of my life.

Before pushing the syringe into my leg I realized that this is a turning point in my life. Never again will I be at the "pre-injection" phase. This is an idiosyncratic construct but it signals my acceptance of "my condition." I can't will it away or ignore it and expect an easy resolution. Injecting medicine is serious business.

Truthfully, I'm very grateful that help exists and is available. I just didn't want to be someone who needed it. But, as Nancy said, in our 60s, we all have something. I am encouraged that my illness is known and treatable. I will use all the support that the medical profession offers but I take my healing as my responsibility. I commit to nurturing my healing consciousness. I am aware that Source knows my needs. I also know that Source offers me direction and support every day. I need to listen carefully to discern the specifics. And I need to receive and not to think. Thinking obliterates Source's message.

June 23

I walked on the treadmill for 30 minutes yesterday, Sunday, when the gym doesn't open until 8:00. Then I used a few machines instead of swimming. I appreciate the alternate exercise which is hard to fit in on days I swim.

Walking on the treadmill for 30 minutes is harder than swimming for 65 minutes. I hold onto the side rails constantly. When I first started walking on the treadmill, my arms ached. Now I try to hold on lightly but I still don't have the balance to let go altogether.

Three friends with whom I've walked the last two months have allowed me to lean on their extended arms when I've needed extra support after the initial twenty minutes. Of course, I always use a cane when I go out for a walk. The neurologist asked me at our second meeting if I am using a cane more and I replied (somewhat diffidently), "No." Morning walking is fine and a cane slows me down. Holding a purse, car keys, a wallet, opening a door, and carrying my briefcase are all I can handle. I don't really need a cane until mid-afternoon when I tire more easily. I enjoy the energy of the morning hours.

In the mornings, I arise at 4:30, do floor exercises, drive to the pool, swim, return home, eat, meditate, and rest. Then my work day starts. I see Medicare clients in their homes for individual psychotherapy. I began serving this population when I moved to this area. Very many folks need services but can't easily leave home. I don't want to maintain an office so our needs mesh nicely. I see adults who are challenged physically by normal aging in addition to those confronting unexpected situations. They are folks who have lived with integrity making decisions that seemed like good judgment at the time they made them but life still led them down an unexpected alley. And there are the folks whose impulses historically have ruled them, now living with diminished options and capabilities. Both groups find themselves up against one or more walls, uncomfortable and confused.

At this time in my life I am surprised, also. During my initial hospitalization in 1971 the neurologist said I would age more quickly than others. The last nine years (since menopause at 55) have thrust me into my senior stage with a fury. Consequently, I have eliminated all needless running around. I think about where I must go, the parking, and my energy level. I don't go out in the evening because I'm too tired. I rest every day, sometimes sleeping. I'm satisfied with less activity.

I've lost a lot of busyness but I've gained a deeper level of acceptance, both of myself and of others. Now I appreciate whatever there is to appreciate about folks I encounter. I'm not driven and not goal-oriented. That involved a major shift and a surrender. I know I can't effect what I want so I delight in the gifts I receive.

In my meditation yesterday I was led to post a giveaway on craigslist — my mother's 1948 Singer sewing machine. I had taken it out of the carrying case the day before and discovered it doesn't work. (It had been more than twenty years since I had used it but I thought maybe . . .) Within three hours of posting the ad a young woman picked it up and left a cute Thank You note. She needed a part for another 1940s era machine which can't be bought and was delighted to receive mine. Source had orchestrated the transfer precisely.

When Source works its magic around me and with me, I feel great joy. That's how I participate in life.

June 28

Yesterday was my second injection, my first solo trial. It went fine; no big deal. I knew what to expect and handled it without emotion, quickly and easily. This afternoon I feel the "flu-like" symptoms previously advertised so I've rested. Resisting is useless. It also shows me how much I have driven myself to be active all my life. There was always a new goal; I felt uncomfortable if I weren't achieving in some way.

Now I can't force anything. So I feel the anxiety and continue resting. What else can I do?

I'm not inviting friends to walk anymore. I just decided that. My gait isn't improving as I had hoped. I'm considering the wisdom of accepting my limitations. That would be totally unlike me but the physical evidence is what it is. I can speak optimistically but my leg weakens after twenty minutes. It's happened repeatedly.

I saw the neurologist yesterday. He had seen me walk on the treadmill in the gym and told me that was ill-advised. He said I'm not exercising for endurance but to strengthen the smaller muscles on the outside of my thighs. He asked if I were still seeing the physical therapist. He said not to get too tired or too hot and not to overdo the exercise. Apparently, I have only "old folks" goals now.

But what can I say? It sounds like a relief. He is giving me the reprieve my mind won't. So my mind is left with, "Can I trust Source to take care of me as well as I want?" That sounds stupid and egotistical and immature and selfish. My fear is that I will be forgotten. Source shows me dozens of times a day that I'm not forgotten but still the ancient fear lives.

This morning I arose later than usual since it's Saturday and the gym isn't open early. I felt extremely anxious. I meditated for an hour before leaving but the anxiety persisted. I was facing a weekend without plans. I can get so depressed without contact and here I was expecting no contact for two days. On the road to the bottomless pit.

But my friend Antoinette emailed a note saying she'd drop by at 11. She did, bringing the vegetable soup she makes. Twice a week she gives me vegetable soup. A kinder or more generous offer I can't imagine. Since I don't cook, food is always a challenge. I need to be very careful about my diet and she provides all the healthy, delicious vegetables I need. She's truly an Earth Mother and I love her.

We sat in my garage with the door open, enjoying the beautiful day. We talked and laughed for more than two hours. She's a realtor in business for herself and has lots of tales which intrigue me. Our time together couldn't have been more perfect. Exactly what I needed and wanted. And my mind didn't make it happen. Thank you, Source. Why do I doubt?

June 29

"I am healthy, happy, and strong." This is my new affirmation. My healing is completely personal. My choice to experience joy and to embrace life will help me walk more than doing additional physical exercises.

By nature I tend toward depression. The Enneagram identifies me as a 4. Characteristic of 4s: a longing to be special but a belief in their own flawedness, an identification with the Victim, a resistance to being happy, and difficulties in relationships. Of course, 4s heal and their great depth offers insight to the other types.

I value the specific gifts of the 4. I will go to any depth inside me to know who I am. I observe others resisting their feelings, choosing to be numb instead. I would no more choose numbness than I would choose suicide, which actually seems very similar. I don't understand opting for comfort instead of embracing honest feeling. I want to know, understand, and experience every detail of my inner world.

I don't like superficial contacts. When someone holds me at a distance, not opening to being known but wanting my attention, I feel insulted. "Either practice presence or leave me alone," I want to shout. I value intimacy and I search for connection. Historically, I've not been good at either with the exception of doing individual psychotherapy. There I love to watch and play with the unconscious. The beauty and specificity and wisdom of the deepest parts of ourselves inspire me. Doing psychotherapy always yields an experience of Source at work/play. I need that.

At this point in my life when physical healing is my focus, I embrace healing at every level. I surrender to Source's wisdom. I state my intention — to walk perfectly. I trust and I release. I don't know how it will unfold nor is it my job to orchestrate the details. By asking and aligning with the vibratory frequency of the Universe, I am guaranteed to receive my good.

And I allow healing psychodynamically. I release all old hurts and resentments. I practice forgiveness and appreciation. I hold no resistance inside. Doing my own psychological work is the best I can do to heal. I allow healing when I choose to move into the place of experiencing vibrational health. Words and affirmations don't matter unless they are anchored in a new reality. Then they serve to remind me of the existence of that reality. But without offering a new vibration, words are meaningless. Practicing a healed vibration heals. And that means being me without limits. I only need to practice presence and allow the Universe to pull me to healing. My job is to be me fully. That's all that is important. Not being better than I am or being different or being more. Just being myself 100%. That's why I'm here. To be myself. And that's all I need do.

June 30

It occurs to me that I can adopt an attitude of joy and appreciation for my chronic condition. Maybe I don't need to resist it. Maybe I will say, "Good to see you and welcome." Maybe I'll embrace life through its eyes.

For some reason it is important that I experience this chronic condition. So I will. Fully. Open-heartedly.

Why not? It is here and it is mine. I won't focus on resenting it or pushing it away. I will say, "What is my gift in accepting you?"

Surrender takes on a new meaning in this context. A chronic condition is not a problem to be solved. It is my life. For now.

Now I experience me differently. Now I adopt an attitude of awe. This chronic condition isn't awful; it's awe-filled. My body expresses Source. And it's declaring definitely to my mind, "I will not be ignored and I will not be controlled."

Surrender is saying, "Yes." To everything I experience. "Yes" to my body no matter how it operates. "Yes and I love you." No more pressure, no judgment, no criticism. "Yes" to life no matter how life looks or feels. "Yes and I appreciate this second and today." I want to experience this chronic condition with gentleness and acceptance and humor.

After all, who knows how long chronic is?

July 2

My inner world is amazing. A day or two before I clearly receive an insight, I'm unfocused and anxious. I notice that I overeat and miss sleep. My routine deteriorates.

The clarity comes when I'm not focusing on myself. I'm swimming or driving or watching television and the issue becomes clear. I experience an emotional awakening, complete with feelings belonging in the past. Suddenly, I see how the current situation re-creates an old unhealed one. Staying in my Adult, I can watch it resolve in the present. What a relief. And a surprise. It's all about allowing.

Although I'm currently focused on physical healing, I'm getting lessons about giving and receiving love. Admittedly, they are terrific, just unexpected. The love thing has always frustrated me. Relationships of every kind have challenged me. Finally, at 50 I surrendered. I moved to a small town, I practiced stillness. I told myself I would accept solitude. It was a relief to not resist. And a surprise that loneliness doesn't come from being alone.

I learned that my attitude toward myself had more impact on my experience than other folks' behavior. While previously I had expected my feelings to be changed by what happened to me, I learned that my feelings create what happens to me. The movement is from the inside out. I learned that I can spend much time alone and have it be exhilarating or depressing depending upon which subpersonality talks to me. My Inner Critic wants me dead and tells me so loudly. If I allow her to go on and if I believe her, I head down a self-destructive path. If I turn around and confront her and stay in my Adult, I am empowered.

It's all about the inner work. The world I experience is different from the world anyone else experiences because my inner world is different from theirs. I can't help them because they are creating their experience from inside as am I. That's why meditation is so important.

I'm relying on meditation for my physical healing. I'm inspired to offer open meditation groups every day at noon at my house. I want to uplevel my practice and meditating with others helps so much.

July 7

Is 7-7 significant? Today feels like the start of a new chapter. My new clients were good for one session. My old clients are disappearing. That leaves me staying here and meditating.

We had six folks at the group today. It was great. They left and I napped. What's wrong with that?

Elissa gave me the most beautiful card I've ever received. She compared me to Oprah as far as bringing good things into her life. The job I recommended worked out. The new employer called me and said they like her. She said she likes them. And she said, "It was so easy."

She had hung out in their neighborhood near the ocean and fantasized about living there. I love her excitement and appreciation and joy. I was key in creating this job and getting her involved. Was I operating from inspiration? Felt like it. Certainly it couldn't have been better for everyone.

That makes me feel like I truly am operating in partnership with life and that's thrilling. It also lets me know I can trust my intuition. So I will trust my intuition that now my job is to meditate.

July 8

"I am one who loves unconditionally."

I heard those words in an Abraham/Hicks YouTube video today. Abraham encouraged the listener to clean up her vibration by aligning with Source. Abraham said it was possible to match Source vibration in 30 days by releasing resistance.

I am thrilled to hear this. That's all I need to do, I know that. That is the key to my physical healing, my emotional healing, my relationship fulfillment, and my joy. Abraham calls it expansion. I call it life. I want this so much.

Now that I can see how close I am, I will trust it and enjoy it. I will see myself, down the road, already walking, I will love unconditionally because that heals me. It isn't about getting others to change. It's about me changing. I learned that in the drive back from San Diego last weekend. It's all about my attitude. I don't need to evaluate how well my walking is doing, I just need to keep doing the work.

I was impressed with how patient I was on the trip. I want to keep that patience and allow.

July 10

Speaking with my friend, Karen, I described my overwhelming feelings of love for Rob, now 17. I met him as an infant when he lived next door. One day his mother carried him as I walked toward them. He reached out to me and I held him. "That's the first time he's ever done that," his mother said. At that second, something in my heart shifted and immediately I loved him.

When I saw him last week I felt the same flood of emotion. I've not felt that before and never for an adult. I adore Rob and, although he's a great person, my reaction is totally without reason. Something instinctual exists in me towards him. I don't know that it's reciprocal.

Karen said, "You experienced what it's like to be a mother." I guess so. The love is boundless. And it scares me a bit. I trust this isn't a coincidence, feeling a depth of love I haven't known at this time when healing my body is uppermost for me.

I saw the physical therapist today and we focused on core exercises. The first decline I noticed at menopause was that I couldn't tuck my hips under. After that, many other losses ensued. One by one I have regained abilities I lost in the order that I lost them but I haven't been able to force or to choose to tuck my hips under. Now I can feel that happening. I can effect it for a few minutes consciously but I also notice that it is happening without my attention.

Is this connected to loving Rob? To loving? Is my heart experience connected to my walking?

July 11

Today I went downtown. I found a parking place and walked to the shop I needed. That sounds mundane and it is. I am overjoyed to want to do something mundane and to actually do it. I didn't feel sick. I wasn't limited by fatigue or pain. I didn't use a cane. And I wanted to do something to improve a little piece of my life.

This is such a change in attitude — an opening, a diminishment of a low-level depression. I have felt so limited physically and so lacking in hope. These last weeks and months I have received such support and involvement from so many folks. It really destroys my sense of solitude.

I had reached a point where I couldn't help myself any more. Others appeared and truly have helped. I feel better than I have in years. I have hope I will continue to feel better and stronger.

July 13

This chronic condition necessitates lots of rest. Yesterday was a great day — my walking felt easier, I laughed with a friend at lunch outside. Life doesn't get better.

Today I feel the effects of yesterday's weekly dose of meds and I just want to rest. I did shop for a swimsuit, a minorly traumatic experience in a small dressing room with a large, close mirror. It makes me want to cycle in the gym to firm my legs. But the reality is that no matter how much my Controller wants me to take action, I am limited. I have learned that when I rest, I recover. I don't know how much rest is required or how long recovery will take, but I have no other choice.

My Controller has appropriated Sunday mornings when I can't go to the gym early. I arise at 4:30, wash the sheets, do some housework, replace the sheets, maybe wash a load of clothes, and catch up with the papers on my desk. I leave for the pool for a 1/2 mile swim at 7:40. I'm at church before 10 but feel myself getting drowsy during the service. Now that I have the meditation group at noon, I come home and shift my focus but stay alert. A nap follows sometime in the afternoon but my Controller wants to do something with the day.

This second-half of life is not for my Controller to dominate. She's done her best but her day has past. She hasn't accepted that entirely.

Any glimmer of relief and she perks up. My challenge is to use her in small and short ways and to constantly practice allowing. Always I need to be anchored in the present second, paying attention. Why is that so hard to accept? It feels like a loss but a wise loss. Surely, I have learned something from all my years of driving myself. Why resist wisdom?

July 15

I realized in a quiet moment this morning that my fingertips no longer go numb when I swim. It was happening at each swim and it was bothering me. I prayed, asking for healing. The numbness hasn't happened in a while but I didn't notice that it had resolved. My prayers were answered, slowly over time, when I was distracted and not thinking about my concern.

That's how healing works. Slowly, gradually, but effectively. And without input from my Controller after the initial request.

The Abraham/Hicks model is:

1. I request.
2. Source says, Yes.
3. I must allow in order to receive.

Clearly, allowing is all I need to practice. Source hears my every request. Source always responds affirmatively, immediately. I must release resistance to receiving.

Releasing resistance happens on every level. Resistance to feeling feelings? I must release it and feel them. Resistance to accepting another? I must release it and accept her and appreciate her just as she is in the moment. Resistance to accepting myself unconditionally?

I must release it. I can't have an opinion. I can't think or judge or evaluate. My challenge is simply to be present and to allow Source to heal me.

Like opening a dam, I allow.

July 18

The home health care nurse visited yesterday to teach me how to use the second and forever (weekly) injection device. According to her, less than 1/4 of those with my diagnosis have access to the medication which will slow the progression of the disease. It's unbelievably expensive but agencies fund it. Getting the information about how these distribution and funding systems work challenges everyone, medical professionals and patients alike. After several months I have a workable system in place to receive the drug and have it paid for by a funding agency. One drug in place, one more drug to go.

I am very, very fortunate. I am receiving more support than I realized. The home health care nurse committed to be my advocate, available to intervene any time I ask. Apparently, I am participating in leading edge drug treatment. And it's paid for. More reason to be grateful and then even more grateful.

July 19

Today I feel hopeful. I've had so many Controller lessons this year. And they have all shown me my inner relationships — my Child and My Controller, my Adult and my Controller, my Spiritual Seeker and my health. I know I can heal myself. Rather, I know that when I maintain a vibration at Source level, healing will manifest on every level.

I was wondering what vibration I needed to experience and in my meditation yesterday with Antoinette I got it — to love myself. The love I feel for Rob was my picture of the love I need to always maintain for myself. The Controller taught me to hate myself and to feel good about it.

The Controller isn't evil; I just gave her work outside her area of competence. She applied her same thinking and evaluative skills (which are great for paperwork and taxes and car maintenance) to the project of making my life a success and making me safe. There's no way she knows how to find joy or peace but she did what she knows — criticize and judge.

In my contacts with Controllers this year, I've accepted them, seen their pain, and appreciated what I could. I've stayed in my Adult and allowed. It has been restorative and healing. And I've marveled at myself going through these interactions. Where did the patience come from? I've not been able to do that before but this year it has worked so well. Feels like help from Source.

The Universe is always communicating with us. When I state my intention to heal, the Universe immediately says, Yes. Then I need to pay attention to receive my guidance. The Universe will show me how to heal but I need to stay out of my head (the Controller's arena) and be available. I need to maintain a vibration of expectancy and trust that what I request, already is. I need to know myself healed.

This makes absolute sense to me. I can't share it with the medical professionals, though, or really with anybody else. Now I just need to do the work to love myself, to know myself healed, and to pay attention and allow. Paying attention is crucial. It's so easy to fall into the well-established habits of Controller thought or old self-pitying feelings. Whatever is familiar is suspect.

When I lead guided meditation groups I instruct participants to look at their thoughts. I wonder if most of them know what I mean. Our thoughts are like wallpaper. We think we see *what is* instead of realizing that *what is* inside us informs how we see. Getting into our essential core allows us to see the fallacy of our assumptions but if we identify with our thinking we never get there. And we don't even know that our thinking/minds/Controllers sabotage us. We all like to think we can trust our minds and we can — but only in the most petty, detailed terms.

As far as eternal life and being and Source energy, our minds undercut us and don't even feel bad about it. They do their jobs and won't let go until we detach adequately to view them in their antics. They operate like little wind up toys and keep chugging along until we don't pay attention to them any longer.

In the face of this challenge my mind has offered suggestions about exercising but apparently I can't do what my mind requires. Exercising (more than swimming) just weakens my body. I can only sit and look at the contents of my thoughts and my feelings. I can practice a higher vibration, far from my Controller, into my deepest core. I can choose joy. I can trust and know my healing even though I don't understand each precise step to it. But what is essential for me now is to **be** — with integrity and with presence and with knowing.

When I escaped my lease in Santa Barbara and moved back to San Luis Obispo county, I felt such strength and total commitment. I knew exactly what I wanted and when I wanted it to happen. Every detail fell into place, without any choreography on my part.

That's how I choose to live the next months. I see myself walking perfectly. I feel my appreciation for myself. I forgive everyone and really have no need to hold onto any uncomfortable feelings. I make no one wrong. I learn from everything. I know my best comes to me now. I am glad I have the opportunity to heal with this condition. That's better than not having it at all!

July 20

This morning at church, Leona asked us each to share what we do to contribute to peace. Of course, at Unity we know that peace starts inside. I spoke about my commitment to healing. This morning I walked vertically (not so bent over) from my house to the corner and back again. The first time in nine years I could maintain good posture.

I have been doing my core exercises and could feel my hips tuck under "naturally" which keeps my back straight. But in addition to the physical details, Source is involved. My healing is happening now while I focus on practicing vibrational integrity, while I facilitate a guided meditation group every day, while my Controller issues heal.

I am pleased and optimistic. The congregation applauded in support of me. This has been such a solitary journey that having others acknowledge me and truly understand how I'm approaching my healing warms my heart. Healing on another level.

July 22

My experience today illustrates the power of the momentum of thought. I drove to a new client's home 20 minutes away from my home. I felt irritated and pessimistic about her before I met her. The phone conversation with the client and her caregiver to arrange the initial appointment was distorted and confused. I had decided we probably would not work together well and that this trip was really a waste of my time.

Even though the caregiver's directions were fine, I couldn't follow them. I didn't turn at the stop sign as she had specified, rationalizing that it wasn't the correct stop sign. I drove around for twenty minutes, growing increasingly lost. I anticipated calling her and saying I couldn't find the house so we can't meet. When I gave up the struggle and headed back toward the freeway, I found the streets that corresponded to her directions and came upon the house in short order.

Our meeting was fine. The client was a lovely elderly lady, confined to a wheelchair with no hope of improvement with her chronic pain. Of course, she is depressed. But I know how to practice presence in an apparently hopeless situation and was glad to sit with her.

My petty mood on the way over was infantile, needless, resulting from self-defeating thoughts. I had felt so "on track" all day but lost my sense of guidance when my mood interfered with my being present. When I lost the bad mood, all worked out well.

If I were in the client's position, 80 something with chronic pain, confined to a wheelchair, I would also be depressed. In my life it's just my Controller whining. That's not depressing; it's just stupid and irresponsible. I want to watch my mood more carefully and choose a wiser course.

With my daily 45 minute meditations I'm seeing how my outer world experience reflects my inner world experience in the second. No delays, no mistakes. Whatever I'm feeling shows around me. I am definitely creating my own reality.

July 23

The latest Controller in my life (in an apparently never-ending line of Controllers) is a new client. Getting acquainted, we spoke frankly about her inner world, especially about her Controller who drives her. She also acknowledged her sad and hurt Child. She stated that she wishes to avoid the Child's feelings and then continued to describe her panic attacks.

Pretty easily I led her into her Child's sadness and she stayed there and allowed tears. I've never known a Controller to open up so quickly and cooperatively. I take it as a reflection of my inner Controller healing. This new client has an over-developed Controller but she is also capable of relationship and is wise enough to question the dynamics behind her panic attacks. She wants to do her work and acknowledges my input as valuable (although she didn't want to come back for a month).

Having a relationship with my inner Controller has been a lifelong challenge. Mostly I didn't want to have a relationship with her. I didn't want to know her or hear from her. I wanted her incessant criticism of me to stop. With this new client, I'm seeing the Controller as a deeply human figure who is confused. My Controller may cause me pain but she is hurting so much herself underneath her rough exterior. Just as I work with the client to own her feelings and feel them, I need to respect my Controller and help her to mature

That's why there have been so many Controllers in my experience. I've not done well with them but I must do well now with my interior relationship. My inner Controller seems to be the primary figure in distorting my alignment with Source. Her voice is so compelling and her pressure to act/stay busy/do is so familiar.

All these other Controllers over these decades were directing my attention back inside me. I got caught up in making the various Controllers wrong, but they were just showing me myself. I didn't want to acknowledge that I have a giant-size Controller in my head. But I do.

I need to look at her, to see what she is doing. But I need to listen to Source. I need to be inspired, not driven. I need to allow, not perform. Trust is more important than achievement. And being available needs to be my every minute stance.

July 24

I made a call to check about drug #2 and within the hour it was approved. I feel greatly relieved.

I was wondering after meditation today if I'm really doing anything in meditation. The fact that my life is proceeding well would indicate that I am. Abraham says that we need to be in the vibrational vicinity to receive and that that is our greatest work. We ask frequently enough but we don't ready ourselves to receive so what can Source do?

I'm grateful to be this far with the drugs and the co-pay assistance. I will practice staying happy.

July 26

I wrote the August newsletter today:

"Imagination establishes the blueprint for what can happen within time and space. . . Imagination gives the Universe direction. . . Thoughts become things no matter what you're thinking. . .You are here to learn of your power, your divinity, and your sovereignty."

Mike Dooley states these truths in **Choose Them Wisely**. I love that they invite us to live large. We're not here to fit in or to replay our predecessors' lives. We're here to do something that's never been done.

The Universe cooperates with us and assists us because it's a natural law. As Mike says, "The supernatural pull of your thoughts continues long after you think them." We are creators. Our thoughts precede our outer world experience, for better or worse. Always we are creating.

Let's create with a conscious awareness of what we choose.

I've learned in my meditations that at our deepest core we are already healed, already whole, already vibrating at the frequency of Source. We can always choose to experience that vibration or the worry/fret/resist vibration. We are both Source energy and completely human.

No matter what the concern, the answer usually is, "Go to Source." And in that vibration we are unlimited. Of course, we need to practice that unlimited Source vibration and to own it. The more we do so, the more we trust it and the more we live in its rhythm. We learn to expect guidance as we experience it more and more.

The more we vibrate at the frequency of Source, the better life works for us.

The first step is releasing resistance. To vibrate at the frequency of Source we can't be resisting our feelings, judging them, or denying them. We feel them and let them pass without reaction. We can't be resisting our own power. We acknowledge that Source lives in and through us and that "playing small" is just pretending. We can open to power beyond measure.

Let's imagine that. What do you want to see in your life that your mind says, "Probably not"? Do you want to open to that unrealistic possibility, practice the vibration at the level of Source, and invite a miracle? A miracle is only a natural law that our minds won't accept as inevitable. We are so much more than our minds are capable of knowing and we deserve so much more than they tell us to expect.

Let's identify with the essential core in us and allow. Let's practice that often. And let's see what happens!

July 27

Arising at 4:30am on a Sunday seems much earlier than arising at 4:30am every other day. I'm glad I'm in a routine but the rest of the world doesn't meet my schedule on Sundays. Immediately after meditation yesterday I felt myself sink into the old self-loathing pit. The ache is so familiar. I recognize the thoughts but know they are inappropriate. I talk to the Critic and tell her to stop.

The pattern is so deep. Today I watch myself move through it and I realize that that is what I need to do — just keep moving through it. If I don't react, I don't get stuck. So, just move and move and move and with continual movement, it really doesn't matter what any minute's experience is for it will soon pass. It's important not to talk or think or analyze, just to allow the ongoing movement.

That's an effective meditation when it carries me that directly into an unhealed pit. I wasn't feeling anything in particular before meditation but apparently the unseen Healer knew exactly where I needed to go.

So much sadness and shame . . . I exercise; that always helps. I remember Source is not part of the self-loathing and I wonder how long until it passes. Leaving the gym in San Luis Obispo I encounter a young man I usually see in the Arroyo Grande gym. With a huge smile he greets me by name. Something about being recognized touches me deeply. We chatted for two minutes. A young woman holds the door for me as I leave. Two acts of kindness in the midst of terrible intrapsychic abuse. I had to tolerate the abuse but Source wasn't in it. I was allowing healing by letting it pass. I also felt loved. The two folks who were kind to me expressed that love. I don't know if they understand how much their kindness meant on a day I was suffering. Source worked through them. I feel reassured. And healed.

From this powerful experience I have learned that healing for my body happens in my consciousness. I learned that Source will direct the healing by carrying me in meditation where it knows I need to go. I learned that Source will orchestrate the healing and present me with the experiences I need to heal.

Note to myself: be available and allow. The Universe will take it from there. Pay attention and don't think.

July 30

Healing profoundly is the only thing that makes me excited and motivated about committing to participating passionately in the rest of my life. This project is worthwhile.

It requires a vibratory shift, owning that I'm a winner, staying out of the past, releasing anger, allowing the Victim/Child to mature, owning the Hero vibe. I commit to doing something no one else has ever done. I love that.

In meditation today I saw the fear behind my Controller. So much Controller stuff goes on inside that I don't see. The fear — can I be happy, can I use my time in a gratifying way, can I live meaningfully? The attitude of walking in partnership with Source and trusting life to present opportunities to me makes more sense than anything else.

This project is totally vibrational. Part of me wants to convince Source to help me but in reality Source has already said Yes and knows exactly the healing I need. I know I can trust that. (I feel a wobble when I say that so I need to practice that vibe.) If I know it, Source knows it. I want to practice that confident vibe more.

I know I can do this. It was inspiration to hold daily meditation groups; they have been powerfully healing for me. I want to convince myself and Source that Source should be with me but I don't need to do that. That's still coming from a belief in my powerlessness but the truth is in owning my power. I don't have limitations. Of course, I can do this. Owning that vibe. Knowing my power. Celebrating my power. Trusting my healing. Knowing that my partnership with Source is strong and not giving into that powerless afraid Child who-always-feels-lost vibe. Truly, I know that I am a winner and I will win big in ways no one has seen. I know I can do this. And I want to do something of this magnitude. I like this challenge. I accept this challenge. I'm very glad to have this challenge.

An interesting note: all my life I haven't been confident. It seemed forbidden and wrong. What if now my healing depends upon my being super-confident, owning that Hero vibe, knowing that I can do what no one else has? I must believe in myself — something that wasn't allowed in my youth. I was rewarded for being depressed and other-oriented. Now it feels like I must be over-the-top confident and sure of what I want and completely trusting of myself. I need to be singly focused. No room for depression or doubt or wondering or whining. Just know I am a winner. And proceed.

That's a total turnaround. My Controller is offering her derision and her reality: "This dream isn't realistic." I know it's not. That's why I like it and why I embrace it. It's not ordinary or mundane or commonplace. It's extraordinary and that's what I want for my life — something extraordinary. Since the meditation this afternoon I feel clear and confident. I will watch for signs of my Controller's sabotage in this worthwhile project.

August 1

Some firsts:

— My health insurance deductible has been met and the insurance is paying some expenses. First time in my life. Thank you, Obamacare.
— Today was my best meditation ever — no thoughts but a strong sense of peace and ease.
— I know clearly that the Universe is supporting me. We will do this.
— I'm releasing anxiety and self-destructive beliefs. Now is the time to do my life my way.

August 6

I watch myself make changes. Last week I bought clothes unlike what I usually wear. I've altered my swimming to include more water aerobics and fewer laps. Sleep eludes me even when I'm very tired.

I noticed when a friend described her Critic's sabotaging interventions that I wanted to say, "Why don't you tell your Critic to buzz off?" This morning I realize I'm seeing myself. I've wondered about suicide as a way to escape my Critic's relentless hateful messages but why haven't I told her loudly to be still? She deserves my fury. In response to outer world adversaries I've not been able to fight back or even to feel the rancor necessary to launch an attack. I could rationalize my passivity, but the truth was I couldn't do otherwise. That's how my father was. He would get so angry but it all went inside. I know that frustration.

It's so clear that my Critic is wrong. No doubt she's just misguided and needs my help to learn and grow but I don't care about helping her right now. I just want her to leave me alone and to stop pulling the rug out from under me. I like that metaphor because that is exactly how it feels. I think I'm anchored but then the ground shifts.

I'm tired of feeling bad about myself. I'm tired of the self-hate. I'm tired of trying to be different and hoping someone notices and approves. I'm tired of doing what I've been doing and I choose something different.

These wallpaper issues are based upon assumptions it's hard to question since they are hard to see. What I've always believed has led to poor self-esteem but it's so basic that it requires a radical shaking free at the base to even notice my foundation cracks.

I have remained identified with my passive Child way beyond the time that was appropriate to release. I don't need to hold onto her old feelings. Now I can take care of myself and I can use my words to establish my boundaries. I am respected in the world. Now I can form a good life for myself. I don't need my Controller, the manufactured figure who steps in to stop the action when my Child is prominent, instead of my Adult.

I don't need to feel intimidated or afraid or unsure that Source is with me in this, the biggest project of my life.

I've had a pattern of not quite making it to the end of projects successfully. I start well enough but I peter out before I reach a satisfying conclusion. Well, not this time. Now I believe in myself or rather I trust in my alignment with Source. I know that Source believes in me and that Source is with me. Source always has been but my Controller has blocked Source. When I doubt or expect abandonment, I'm not fully present. But those are the accrued subtle wallpaper dynamics built upon decades of experience with other humans which trip me up.

Source loves me entirely, without restrictions. Source is willing to partner with me in the project of healing myself. My doubt will cancel that partnership. I need to proceed knowing that all is well and I am well and I am what I want. See the final truth. Know it real now. Practice the winner vibe. Let my Controller retire. Forget all those outer world controllers. No more criticism. No more antagonism, no more hate. I am a winner and my knowing that is all that counts.

This is especially important for me to know now since my walking isn't improving. I can't see the path to perfect walking though I affirm that. I do see improvement in my alignment and my inner world equilibrium. I'm trusting that Source is working in ways I don't see. The new medication comes tomorrow. I am hopeful. I trust Source's unseen plan. I focus on vibrational reality and not manifest reality.

August 7

This morning I started my swim cautiously. While stroking I realized I could pull hard under the water and lift gently above the water. My shoulder is still healing and I don't want to re-injure it. The strength used to pull felt energizing, the gliding felt smooth. I enjoyed the exercise. The more I swam the better I felt and then the endorphins kicked in. At the end of the swim I had done a mile in record time (for me) and I felt great. I was friendlier in the locker room and confident. I remember when exercise used to boost my confidence. Everything is better with endorphins.

I also feel more confident about life. My shoulder is healing well and I prayed for that. I am trusting that other healing is coming. With more exercise I feel less neurotic. That's majorly helpful.

I feel optimistic this morning and confident. My Controller is doing a good job keeping the house neat which is her appropriate task. Having her out of my head helps me feel better and helps the house look better. I'm giving away much stuff tomorrow. Letting go of burdens. I don't know how this started but I think the daily meditations contribute. It will be so much fun to see the manifestations in my walking. I know that's coming. I will enjoy the process.

August 12

The new medication is great. I take it twice a day. My walking is more normal. My leg feels like a leg. I can move it more easily. My body doesn't have the "gaps" in functioning. A miracle. I am truly grateful and a bit overwhelmed. A wonderful gift.

August 13

I wrote next month's newsletter article today:

"Your ancestors want to be remembered as they are now, not as they were in human form." Abraham responded to questions about the wisdom of our ancestors by elucidating that they live now, that we maintain a relationship with them now (and they with us), and that they have continued to grow and expand after physical death.

What a relief! If you felt anger toward someone that lasted after their death, you can realize that your relationship with them has changed. With death, according to Abraham, we release resistance. We lose the conflicts and defenses and obstacles to our being Essence. That parent/relative/acquaintance you couldn't handle in his lifetime now has lost his obnoxious qualities. You may still resent him for being a jerk to you years ago, but actually now he isn't a jerk in his Essence. And he doesn't even care that you still resent him. He loves you. Regardless of what you say to him or what you think about him, he loves you because that is what he does. Now he is Essence and he exudes Essence.

You may ask, Did he turn into Source? At our core we are each Source. We overlay that pure Essence with our human experiences and resistances and attempts to elude our being but with death all that evaporates and we are left with being who we truly are — Source.

So, your relationship with your deceased nemesis needs to reflect that resolution. Now he probably is exactly as you would have wanted. He probably didn't like being a jerk as much as you resented it. His limitations hurt you and hurt him.

Now he isn't a jerk and you need to acknowledge that and be open to a relationship with a supportive, loving, compassionate figure. Will you do that? Some folks call that forgiveness. I prefer to call it recognizing growth and allowing.

According to Abraham, our ancestors are focused on us as we live today. They think our thoughts and sing our songs. They are not relegated to a distant time and space. The live through us.

There really is no struggle. At this point we all pull in the same direction. Can you accept their love and attention? Do you want to acknowledge that they are with you? Do you want to release your resistance to being Essence before you die? How much of Source do you want to include in your daily life? Can you handle having everything you want and losing your victimhood/your resentment/ your anger? How much good do you deserve? Source and your ancestors want all the best for you. Are you open to that?

August 14

Almost everything seems easier. Seven women came to meditation today. My talks with three stressed folks went well. (If I were young I would have tensed and jumped into action. Instead, I just saw the best for each of them and knew their good is coming.) I told Cuesta College I didn't want to get a TB test and finger prints to offer the Enneagram class and they said I didn't need to.

Being old feels great in some ways. I actually don't think of myself as old but I notice that others do so I play along. Part of being old is losing the emphasis on the physical aspects and tuning into non-physical reality. I live intuitively more than I ever have. It's great fun.

August 16

It's been a week since I started the new meds. I'm noticing an improvement in my vision, clearer thinking, and subtle physical alignment. My right shoulder turned inward with all the physical weakness and now I notice that at times it seems to want to pull back. Of course, that helps me stand straighter. As I stand straighter, I walk better. I look for indications of improved walking and notice that I can walk a little in the evenings, having given that up a few weeks ago. Mostly I know that I am improving and I know that I will continue to improve.

At meditation today I spoke with a frequent attendee who is confronting physical concerns. She told me about a healer who laid hands on her and her symptoms disappeared temporarily. She added that she knew it was her mind. Thinking about it afterward, I realize that he was vibrating at a healing level and upset her vibrations. Her mind has much momentum and restored her old less-than-healthy vibrations in time. I wonder if I were shown that because I need to look at what my mind is doing.

Of course, the answer is yes. Everything is for my benefit. So how does my Controller sabotage me these days?

When I think about the past, especially frustrations, it's my Controller.

When I resurrect old anger instead of letting it dissipate, it's my Controller.

When I think and plan and strategize and make life a problem to be solved, it's my Controller.

When I trust and allow and let life guide me, it's Source.

When I relax and enjoy the day, it's Source.

August 18

I write so many words about my Controller that I wonder if I'm really getting her significance. I paint her as an evil figure, looming over me, subtly destroying my confidence and my life. Clearly, she is not that. She is me. She just feels adversarial to me.

How did I let a natural part of me grow into a monster? How would she feel about being called a monster?

Adult: Well, how is it for you having me see you as unwelcome and the source of my pain?

Controller: You are not taking responsibility. You make me the bad guy but you asked me to protect you.

Adult: I hurt so much from your indictments.

Controller: Let's tell the truth. You don't hurt that much from me now. In fact, you use me as you want and I do a good job for you. When you wanted me to inflate, I did. Now you have deflated me. Stop with the whining. I am not the problem here.

Adult: You're right. I'm having trouble identifying the problem and I so want to.

Controller: Maybe there isn't a problem. Maybe this is life when you are not identified with your powerless Child.

Adult: Yes, it's that identification that necessitates the need for a Controller to hide behind.

Controller: You asked for protection, you got it. Are you ready to feel all your feelings now?

Adult: Absolutely, I am.

Controller: Then use me for details. Stop blaming me.

Her point is that if I fully embrace my life experience, passionately and without reservation, I won't use her inappropriately. That is so true. She developed and grew when I wanted to limit my experience of my feelings but I don't need to do that now.

I need to trust that my days will be meaningful. I need to allow the powerless Child to grow up. The intensity of my feelings has always made it easy to identify with them, even when I tried not to. But now my feelings come and pass and I go on. I don't need a Controller to limit my feelings and I know I'm not powerless.

Knowing I'm not powerless comes from my Source partnership and trust in Life. Especially since I've been meditating daily with the group, I feel aware of and close to the currents of my days. I respect the flows and I honor their wisdom.

So, I won't beat up on my Controller any longer. She did just what I asked. And she's right, she's not a problem. Life as an Adult isn't about problem solving but about growing to meet challenges. She doesn't help me do that but I don't need her to. I have everything I need. When I move into my powerless Child I forget that; I fear, and I start thinking (using my Controller inappropriately).

I had missed that subtle step of fearing. The truth is that Life will show me how to move through my challenges. I am not alone and I am not forgotten.

Note to myself: Remember you are powerful beyond imagination. As long as you stay in your Adult and allow.

August 25

This morning when I left at 5:15, I found a large feather on the steps. For weeks I have been finding small white feathers. They seem like confirmation from Spiritland. On Tuesday I found a larger white feather when Elissa was here. I took it as a confirmation of our working partnership and I gave her the feather. This morning's feather was three times that size. It lay on an outside step with a roof over it, open to the side but not above. Very unlikely it would be there.

I love confirmation from the Universe. I know that manifestations don't happen quickly. I know I will walk perfectly one day. Now I practice knowing my good, trusting, and being happy, not natural for an Enneagram 4. But I will do it because my walking is on the line. In addition to consulting a primary care physician, a neurologist, and a physical therapist, I need to do my psychological and spiritual work in order to walk well.

That is what healing is all about — living in dialogue, asking and receiving, being sensitive to the flows. In the guided meditations I say, "In this second I am attentive and available." That's the way I choose to live — in partnership, receiving and releasing. That is dialogue with Source. Source hears everything I say and think. I don't need to fear that I'm abandoned. With such powerful confirmation, I know Source supports me in my walking. It will happen. Always I will be happy and grateful and attentive.

A new challenge presents itself to me. A newcomer to the meditation group carries a familiar addictive vibe which is apparently still active in me. I recognize the old feelings though I haven't felt them in over a decade. I know how I had acted on them and I'm very clear I cannot do that now. The dichotomy is doing the same stupid acting out I have formerly done vs. staying in my Observer, watching, and allowing healing. And the last step of healing is walking.

The newcomer is a gift for me to be resolute in my commitment to follow Source's guidance. If I must choose between addictive acting out and walking, I choose walking. But above everything, I choose Source. I am committed and attentive.

Walking is the carrot. The work I must do is my own. Healing my longstanding psychological wounds lays a solid foundation. This is a test. I will not fail this test.

August 27

I appreciate the help walking that the new medication affords but the every-night insomnia drains me. I decided it was preferable to feel bad from not sleeping than bad from taking sleep meds that leave me hung over and foggy. That is one challenge.

The heater in the pool broke and for two days I've done a cold 1/2 mile instead of my warm one mile. In the year I've swum there, no interruptions have occurred so I know this is not normal. I hate being cold but they told me in two days the water temperature will be restored. Challenge #2

A third challenge is with an older woman, a client who is depressed. I think she needs the stimulating environment of a residential setting but her daughter is uncooperative. If I push too hard, the daughter resists. If I don't push, the situation doesn't change. I've gathered information on two lovely homes which I will present to them next week. I must treat the daughter respectfully even though she doesn't treat me that way.

Why these challenges/frustrations now? What inside me do I need to consider?

August 28

I am happy this morning. Yesterday I called the daughter who resists me and realized she is afraid. I experience her as controlling. I was withdrawing from her and making her wrong. When I talked to myself, stayed in my Adult, and called her, some block dispersed. I had allowed myself to move into my powerless Child and I projected my controlling Parent onto her. My fear of controlling folks is longstanding but I won't tolerate it anymore.

I actually don't care how I fear at this point. I'm in my final third of life and if I don't confront my fears now, it won't happen. And that thought I won't tolerate. I've been so crippled by my fear. No wonder I have trouble walking!

I wondered if it were an "inspiration" yesterday when the thought occurred to forget the evening medication dose. I already have insomnia and with that being the first side effect of the meds, I was sleeping less. I didn't get tired in the evening and I couldn't fall asleep. I, also, didn't feel rested in the morning after my interrupted sleep. For 19 days I followed the directions for taking the meds thinking the side effects would diminish. Instead I was getting more tired, a little depressed, and feeling uninterested in walking. When a group participant mentioned action he was taking to correct a sleep problem, I decided to take action, too. Then the thought to skip the evening dose. I welcomed sleepiness at bedtime. I fell asleep and awoke intermittently as is my habit. I had slept almost five hours when I awoke at 1:30am. I felt relieved and rested.

Because I felt better for having slept, my swim went better. The pool was colder than yesterday with no one else in it. I asked my Source team, Jeremiah, to help me swim a 1/2 mile. I finished 3/4 mile and received the endorphins (which doesn't happen at 1/2 mile). I was elated.

I still initially think in terms of reward from a Parent for doing good work. I know that isn't the case with Source. But moving out of my powerless Child and into my Adult removed some fogginess which allowed life to happen more easily. It wasn't Source saying, "Good girl." It was me seeing more clearly and accurately. I am so glad I studied psychology and practiced psychotherapy and understand my inner world. The spiritual truths complete the picture beautifully. This is what helps me heal, not focusing on a diagnosis or pathology.

And I do think I notice a slight improvement in my walking since the phone call with the daughter yesterday. Wishful thinking? We'll see.

August 29

Since I haven't slept well since starting the new meds, I altered the med schedule and omitted the evening dose. I have slept much better for two nights but I notice that my walking has declined considerably. I want to walk and I want to sleep. Not sleeping is devastating and I wonder if that is the price for walking. (Of course, if I don't sleep I don't want to walk.)

Panic ensued. Facing a long holiday weekend, I called the neurologist for help with sleeping while still taking the meds. He completely met the vibe I already had going about him and blew me off. I was hurt, frustrated, and angry. I knew I should wait until I am centered and inspired to take action. But I left a message for another neurologist. If it's not meant to be she won't call, I rationalized.

I am practicing my talk for church about unconditional love. Unconditional love is identifying with our Source energy center and viewing the world through those vibes. I approach my recently declining physical situation through a prism of fear and desperation.

I came from a needy Child perspective and was met by an ungiving Parent. I take responsibility for those vibes going on in me.

If I look at the neurologist with unconditional love, I appreciate his diagnosis and his med suggestions. He provided a turning point in my life and offered me hope. Maybe his job is complete. Maybe the next opportunity is to continue with another doctor and build upon the foundation he lay. Maybe he has done all he can do.

I don't want to hate him or be hurt by his reaction. I want to bless him and wish him only the best.

August 30

Yesterday, last night, and this morning I've been somewhere and back again. Friday is my injection day. I did the injection between 4 and 4:30. If side effects occur, it's usually three hours later. Most frequently the side effects have been physical — flu like symptoms. Occasionally, I have noticed a slight depression which has lifted.

Last night I felt the most depressed I've felt in years. It was the familiar hopelessness, the barrel-bottom stuckness, and the overwhelming sense of lostness. All the feelings I've known but I haven't felt with such intensity this decade. The feelings came on fast after the injection but I had been low all day. I was feeling unclear and uncertain. Then in the middle of the night despair draped me. Suicide seemed reasonable and urgent. I've always told myself that if I commit suicide I won't do it impulsively but only after six months of contemplation. Last night I felt a huge push to act quickly.

I knew it was from the drug and that it would wear off and, surely, it did. This morning I swam a mile and felt better. Two women meditated with me at noon. I had sat down early but couldn't generate any momentum on my own. The three of us did a powerful 45 minutes. I am so grateful folks will meditate with me for that reason — the increased power. At the end, I felt centered and accepting and pretty OK. A miracle.

Then collecting my mail I encountered another feather. Yesterday I had asked for a feather but didn't find one. Today a small white feather suspended on an invisible reed fluttered in the breeze, casting a baby shadow. The feather hovered like a hummingbird two inches above the sidewalk. Another miracle.

When I ask for such big gifts as a clear brain MRI next year and total physical healing, I get big challenges. Certainly for the intensity and the pain I went through last night I expect some major unfolding. That's been my experience. In my emotionality it's like a block calcified around old feelings disintegrates and I can be more present in the moment. So when the uncomfortableness comes, I know there will be an opening eventually. I don't understand the pain although an image of an abandoned child came — me when breastfeeding ended prematurely with feelings of overwhelming fear and loss. Maybe that's the basis, maybe not. I'm not going to think about it but I am available to experience my feelings. It's so clear Source is at work. I will follow and trust and come back to the path when I stray into my thoughts. Always I trust.

August 31

The deeper inside I go the more sure it is that I will collide with a wall — the immoveable, dense wall of not believing in my worthiness. Consciously, I am far from that place. But something is holding me back; I suspect this wall.

Not feeling confident, not trusting my spontaneity, not exploding in joy — it's all the same. Old conditioning, learned self-hate, self-imposed limits — all were designed to guarantee safety in the past and all limit me immensely in the present. I choose to let them go. The depression served me at one point but not now. I can't heal completely without releasing it. And knowing that isn't enough.

I must raise my vibratory level. So, I will. Now that I can see the wall, I can dismantle it. And that implies standing up to all those who have disparaged me over the years, whose voices still echo in the caverns of my chest. I will never gain their understanding, let alone approval, and I choose to let them go. I actually don't know what they think of me but I really don't care. I don't even wish them badly. I just want to be free of my self-imposed limitations. And giving my power to ghosts from the past is surely a major limitation.

Sept. 3

I'm getting clearer about the role my Controller plays in sabotaging my healing and the reason for the Controllers in my life. I meditated for 1.5 hours today before I got through my anger. From behind the Observer window I saw a fire floating down the river. I felt a lump in my throat.

What shifted my experience was not identifying with either the Child or the Controller or even the Observer but with the Adult. I don't need to teach the neurologist how to treat folks. I don't think he's interested or open but I can stay in relation to him and still preserve my boundaries.

He sees me as sick. My Controller tells me to be reasonable and points out the fact that I'm not noticing any manifestations of healing. That's true but irrelevant. I need to always firmly, passionately, completely know that my perfect walking comes to me now. I can't have split energy and expect to see my healing.

I've walked around the circle in my neighborhood three times this week. I am walking better. I can see me walking perfectly and, truly, I know that is coming. It's just the Controller who sabotages me. I cannot be reasonable. I must stay true to my vision. Source has said Yes to my request. I must line up vibrationally with Source and with my perfect healing in order to receive it and to experience it. That's my job now. Stay positive, believe in myself, know my own healing. I must maintain a vibrational match to the good I want. And so I must limit my Controller (even if I can't affect the Controllers around me). No matter what anyone says or how anyone treats me I can always believe in myself.

I want to always remember that I am doing leading edge work. It is very solitary at this point. At a time in the future I hope that shifts and others can share this with me. But for now I believe in myself and in Source and in our partnership and the perfect walking that comes now.

Sept. 9

I can feel a shift taking place. I have no idea what's coming. Sunday I spoke at church. The musicians each contributed a piece they very much wanted to share and each performance was stunning. My talk went well. Two folks told me how much love they felt from the group coming toward me. I hadn't recognized that but was gratified to hear it and then to have it confirmed.

My talk was about seeing as Source sees. It was a good talk, I delivered it adequately, it was well received, and the meditation, accompanied by Brett on the piano, was fine. All in all, it felt like a success — a graduation and a wrapping up. I had talked myself out of getting nervous and withdrawing to assuage my Controller. Instead I enjoyed the people there.

I see now that my depression last Sat. (Sept. 6) was meds induced. With time passing, so do the side effects. I don't look forward to Friday nights and Sat. mornings but Sundays always come. Several folks have told me they can see I'm moving more easily. I've felt that and I'm glad it's noticeable. I will practice walking on flat ground today. Clients drift away and I have much free time.

And Elissa left a message about not coming today to clean. It seems that's over, too. She has gotten what she needs from me and may still come to meditation but that feels finished.

I feel minorly elated at the success at this level. I expect my walking to continue to improve but the hard work has been done. The meds will continue just as they are now. All the ground work is laid.

I wonder what's next?

September 10

It occurs to me that I practice resistance by working toward goals. In meditation yesterday I saw that I can appreciate how great the group is right now instead of focusing on a future undetermined date when there will be 50 folks present. Now we have a tight close small group in my living room. The setting is lovely, the folks open-hearted, the experience powerful. What's to criticize?

The guidance to appreciate this moment left me elated and deflated at the same time. Does it mean this is the best it will get? If so, what's wrong with that? Nothing, if I appreciate it. If this is the best my life will ever be and I am dissatisfied and looking to a future date when I will be happy, I am losing this moment. If I am to die next year I want to enjoy and appreciate every moment of today. With a future orientation it's as though I'm saying I will sacrifice today for a huge tomorrow. I will learn by . . . what? Being dissatisfied with today? Pushing myself?

I am so good at pushing myself. Always the future will be better. Always focusing on circumstances. And I know that isn't the answer.

I've felt a change coming and just received a phone call from Antoinette who is sitting with a woman in her office who wants to sell my bags in her shop. Finally, a professional who appreciates my art! Maybe this is the focus for my next phase. Not bad.

Source pays attention.

September 11

I don't think I've ever felt older. Yesterday I attended the first meeting of the county meditation group. I had requested the location because the parking is easy. It wasn't easy yesterday and I walked farther than I had expected. I didn't walk well and it wasn't comfortable.

I am letting go of the hope/dream/belief that I will walk well again. My Controller has been too prominent. I'm recognizing my Controller in ways I hadn't before. I need to practice a new level of surrender. My Controller tells me to consider suicide but after meditation today I felt Norma Spry (a former spiritual teacher now departed) encouraging me to look for gifts I haven't noticed.

Maybe I won't retrieve what I've lost, but maybe this experience will help me open to something more subtle. Maybe I need to grow in ways I can't imagine. Surrender tells me to trust Life. So, surrender. OK. That terrifies me. But I'm clear my walking isn't improving. My meditating is. I'm very grateful to have the support of the daily group.

Back to surrender. No more thoughts of suicide. Committing to be here and to "endure" sounds pretty dreary. I need to allow and to trust and to be available. I can't be the manufacturer of my miracle even though I know what I want. I think I must release it and still be humble and grateful. That seems so sad. But truly not being aligned with the Controller isn't sad; it's being more alive. I'm scared.

September 14

I've felt so tired this weekend that I could sense some discouragement. I evaluate my movement and wonder if I will experience the perfect walking that I affirm. Listening to Abraham this afternoon I realize that I have bumped into a wall. My early belief that I can't have what I want stops this manifestation. In my Adult I affirm my perfect walking but in my unconscious Child I believe I can't have it. Just realizing that opens the doors for me to progress.

Even when I feel discouraged I still see myself walking perfectly. That tells me the discouragement is temporary and the walking is certain. The old belief that I can't have what I need may have been true in the past but it isn't true now. Staying in my Adult and using good judgment, I can have everything and anything.

This is where the Abraham material meets the unconscious. I'm so grateful to have studied psychology and now spirituality and to have a solid meditation practice. I have everything I need to do this work.

September 15

I have moved from depression to anger to release to partnership. I am still in relationship but now I can think as an Adult. It surpasses forgiveness; it's recognizing that I do have the support I need. My work focuses on my consciousness, not on behavior. My walking is improved faster by feeling my feelings, changing my level of consciousness, and experiencing myself differently than it is by doing repetitions of exercises.

I feel happy and optimistic.

September 16

I think the Universe responds to me as I release my layers of defense against my feelings. The days prior I had felt my infancy longing and allowed it. That's all. Just acknowledge it and let it be.

The love I felt coming to me was new. I remember practicing as a child not trusting love that was offered. It was always snatched away, leaving me vulnerable and alone and feeling stupid that I trusted it would maintain. Feeling this new vitality and joy for life was invigorating. Can I trust it? Can I live this way, being happy and undefended and available for more and more good? Can I safely be vulnerable?

I'm guessing Yes. It's worth an experiment. I will be happy and confident that the Universe hears me and will cooperate with me. I have nothing to lose and my life to gain. All the little white feathers I notice around my house reassure me. Living in complete joyful partnership promises a thrilling possibility.

I will do it. I will trust and expect support and gifts. I will appreciate the adventure each day is. I know the Universe watches and cares. And I'm guessing that caring won't be snatched away. Let's see. This week I will notice patterns and consider that things have changed.

September 17

Mostly what I'll do is appreciate. I've never been happier in a healthy way. I finally want to live and enjoy my time on earth. A first.

September 22

I haven't written much lately but I have been alert and practicing. The flow evidences most clearly in emotional terms. The Friday night injections continue to drop me into an intense but short-lived depression. I move into hopelessness and thoughts about death, I recognize that this is drug-induced and that it will pass, and within 24 hours it dissipates. I talk myself through it while watching TV for distraction.

I'm glad I've had so much experience working with my feelings and my inner world. I can recognize my usual patterns and how my feelings affect my thoughts. And, thanks to meditation, I can watch both feelings and thoughts and wait them out. It isn't pleasant but it doesn't last. That's just a fact — taking this medication has side effects. I won't take them personally.

Today after the meditation group the three attendees talked among themselves. The conversation veered to frustration and blaming others. I stopped that immediately. I can't stand to see women choosing a victim role and, when they find themselves in one, I want them to take responsibility.

I know enough about that victim dynamic from decades of experience in my own life. I saw how I was creating it and how I could stop it. I did stop it and I continue to do my work daily.

One woman got it, thanked me, and hugged me on her way out. The other withdrew and walked out while I spoke to her. She just called and, again, hung up while I was talking. She's too rutted in the victim to see what she is doing. So, again I must let go and give her to Source.

When I speak honestly, relationships change. I don't want to be nice, ever. I always want to be honest. I can live with myself then. Many others apparently can't. That's OK.

And so the flow continues. Maybe integrating my anger will help my walking. Seems like I'm pulled to heal on every level. To that I say, YES.

September 24

I feel more anchored in my powerful Adult. I released three folks who apparently don't see reality the way I do. I see how others' lives could change but it's none of my business. I will let the Universe deliver the right folks to me, friends and clients.

When I left the gym this morning, the desk attendant asked if I work in real estate. I referred him to Antoinette. She's ready for business and has been meditating daily with me. Very fun.

While I was with my client this afternoon, her friend who also wants to be a client called. Synchronicity abounds.

Karen gave me a book by TN Hanh about walking meditation. I've read a few pages and somehow it seems magic and healing just to hold it and read it. I also practice the relaxed walking and want to believe I see advantage. Another miracle? We'll see how far the walking improvement goes.

And always there are more feathers.

I feel blessed.

September 27

It occurs to me that I need to consider the Victim role I choose if I notice it and react to it so strongly in others. My thoughts can tend toward the Victim and the past but I catch them and delete. I seem to need to upgrade my avoidance of the Victim and my focus on being the Joyous Creator. Thinking that my Victim obstructs my walking motivates me to choose joy.

My Victim frustrates me as much as others' Victims frustrate me. I can't stand to allow Victim at all in my thoughts; this healing endeavor of mine is all about thought/energy/consciousness.

I noticed some new feelings in my right foot and leg today. It's clear that I need to push down hard with the ball of my right foot to walk better. It allows me to walk taller and to lift my leg more naturally. Otherwise, I'm bending over too much.

I'm going to practice walking harder on the ground. Asserting that I am here. Leaving my footprint. I don't have time to waste.

September 29

I fell on the sidewalk going into church yesterday. It wasn't a bad fall and only a few folks saw me. But it shook me to my core. Is my walking deteriorating? Has Source abandoned me? Have I deluded myself all these months/years believing that healing is possible?

I came directly home and cried intermittently during the day and evening. I fantasized the worst evolving. I felt naive. I despaired. And then I distracted myself.

In the evening, after not thinking much of the afternoon, I realized that the fall was significant because I was at church not because of my walking. At church — where folks support me and seem to appreciate me. At church where I have found a family when I wasn't looking for one. At church where I've been given opportunity after opportunity to practice my craft, to speak, to do workshops. At church where the doors/arms are always open to me. This is the first time in my life when I have felt such acceptance. This church is my first experience of being a wanted part of a group.

I had become accustomed to walking on the outside of any circle, not hoping to be included because I knew I wouldn't be. I had lost hope of deep connection which I've desired more than anything. I have never known what it is to belong.

And, so, my fall was about recognizing the first real family I've had this lifetime — at the church. The fact is my walking is improving and my right foot feels more like a foot than it has in years. I am healing physically as I have prayed for. I didn't pray for healing in my heart but apparently Source insists upon that, also. Healing on all levels.

My back is straighter and lifting my foot is easier. It happened after meditation today. The physical therapy exercises have been great but meditation is miraculous. In a second, doors inside me open and my body wakes up.

Today in meditation I felt like I was a definite and needed part of the flow that carries us all. It was the first time I had experienced that, and a powerful experience it was for all of us. The other attendees acknowledged it, also. I have a place in the world and I'm needed and wanted. I've never felt that. I've not felt the joy and peace that comes with knowing I belong.

That day in April when I encountered Brett in the waiting room after the brain MRI, he suggested that I journal. He asked if I were going to tell the church group about my diagnosis. I thought about it and decided no. My rationale for my customary withdrawal: I wanted to heal myself first so that the brain MRI next spring would be more normal. Then I would announce what I had done.

Falling at church tells me to include my family in my healing now. I don't have to be secretive and I'm not alone. I can ask for their support and their prayers during this healing time. I can trust them. They love me.

October 1

Three weeks ago today the meditation group with the county employees started. I was late, there wasn't a nearby parking spot, I didn't use my cane. The meditation itself went well. Today I was early, there was one perfect parking spot for me, and my walking was great.

October 2

I'm walking more easily and fluidly. I'm tucking my hips under naturally. I'm thrilled. Is this a result of opening my heart and receiving love?

A new client and a new meditator have drifted into my world. Such fun. I expect the workshop on Oct. 4 to be pleasant. In fact, I'm stopping my (Controller) preparations now and practicing light-heartedness.

Immediate manifestations. And probably more are coming.

October 8

Now that I realize how important meditation is to healing and to living, I wonder why I didn't commit myself more fully sooner. I see folks who express an interest but don't follow through by actually meditating. I also see folks who like to talk about meditation as though it were a New Age trend. And I see some folks who are confused about what the meditative process is.

Meditation, for me, facilitates the process of living in partnership with Life. And that is everything. That provides a construct which will answer any question. How to walk again? How to heal? How to maintain nurturing friendships? How to receive money? It's all about partnership and paying attention and trust. Meditation teaches all that.

The diagnosis grabbed my attention. I felt pulled to a deeper level to accept it and deal with it. And I knew I couldn't do it on my own. That must be a major element of partnering with Source. Why practice surrender if I can handle life with my intellect? Maybe that's true for us all. We do what we can and then we hit the wall. When it's clear that I don't have the wherewithal to move forward on my own and I desperately want to, I practice surrender. Source as the final consideration.

I was willing to let go of so much and to live with less and less, until I couldn't give up anything more. Now I want more and more. I want good friends, rooted in their own meditation practice. I want groups of aware folks, doing their work, to eat and laugh with. I want huge money. And I want good sleep. I want it all. And I want it coming now. And it is. I just had to turn around and be ready to receive.

October 9

Returning from my morning swim, I watched the freeway morph into a parking lot. My usual 18 minute drive stretched to a 90+ minute creep. I always have almonds, kleenex, and water with me. This morning I also pulled out of my backseat bag Wayne Dyer's **The Invisible Force**. Randomly, I opened to 149. "The field of intention allows everything to emanate into form, and its unlimited potential is built into all that has manifested — even before its initial birth pangs were being expressed."

Zowee.

Yes, that message is for me. I so want to heal myself or, rather, to allow healing. And, actually, I know that the Universe wants that for me. The Universe would be delighted for me to manifest a healing that hasn't manifested heretofore. The Universe isn't holding me back. In fact the Universe knows me healed right now.

I want to know that, also. I know it in my head. I want it in my heart. I see it in my imagination. It has to manifest. How can it not?

October 11

Vibration precedes manifestation. Reality first is vibrational. If I keep asking for what hasn't manifested I am practicing the vibe of not having, not the clarity of already having. Truly, I know in my soul that I am a person who walks perfectly for as long as I want. That is the vibrational reality inside. I'm not just saying those words. I can feel it. I need to hold onto that reality when my mind starts fretting.

October 12

I'm always testing, looking at how things are going. Lately, I've consciously practiced joy and things are going very well. Joy has been a lifelong challenge. First, my natural personality style isn't light-hearted. Second, I have typically expressed anger by withdrawing. Third, I have noticed that when I feel joy the next step was disappointment so there was a built-in conditioning to not allow trust and joy.

But this week I have really been searching for what will support me in manifesting my goal of walking well. Besides my exercise, I focus on my consciousness. I have chosen joy consciously. And everything has gone well. More interactions with friends. More fun. More sleep. More joy. And today after meditation Claudia stayed and showed me some yoga poses to practice core exercises. Already it feels like the exercises are beneficial.

Additionally, I found a rug online with no tax and no shipping fees.

Life is good.

October 15

I did three 45 minute meditations today with others. This morning I meditated with Ginny at her house. She is confined to the couch with a broken ankle and will reside there six weeks. At noon I meditated with four regulars at my house. Late this afternoon I meditated with eleven county employees. Interspersed, I swam a mile, took a short nap and later a long nap, washed the dishes, walked for seven minutes, and completed two entries for the web site.

A fine day, all in all. I've felt such peace. No need to worry about anything and no need to rush. Maybe this is it. Quiet joy.

October 19

When I review my life I notice how focused I have been in some areas and how passive in others. Despite some lack of planning and poor judgment, I have always done well academically and professionally. A star has lit my way back when I veered off-course. A few well-timed breaks led me to eventual success. It's not all my own doing.

In mid-life when I lost some ability to walk, I accepted it without much resistance. Too many physical challenges hit me at once and I had no support. So, I tolerated greater and greater loss and believed that's just how life was for me. Until I discovered Abraham/Hicks and started working with the Universe.

Universal law governs all of us but I didn't get clear about that until my time off in 2012/2013. It looks like happenstance and coincidence that I was guided to discover a refined and specific spirituality. It certainly didn't hit me all at once and I didn't recognize the magnitude of the shift in my consciousness. Source must have orchestrated my experience precisely. And I've learned that Source always does. We can tune in or not. Our choice.

I'm living one day at a time now and asking for guidance. I trust that the next door will open when I'm ready. I'm given gifts when I don't expect them. After meditation today we stretched. One person showed us a hip stretch that loosened some tightness I've lived with for decades. When I stood my balance and my walking were unsteady as I experienced a new alignment.

That seems like a miracle for me.

October 21

My experimentation with over-the-counter sleep aids continues. I'm taking Ibuprofen PM at 7, Melatonin (3 mg) at 8, another Melatonin at 8:30, and two Ibuprofen at 9. It still takes thirty minutes or more to fall asleep, I awaken three times (or more) during the night, but I get 2-3 hours of solid sleep intermittently. That's new.

The greatest help has been how good I feel during the day. It's like a minor depression has lifted and I'm happy to be alive. I haven't said that often, which embarrasses me and saddens me, but it's true. Mostly I've resisted life and prayed for death. Now I want to live. I feel great about what I'm doing. The county called about another meditation group so I feel recognized and appreciated. Reports from the regular group attendees indicate change happening. One person today wrote me a long email about his insights during meditation. So very confirming.

It's exciting to watch life unfolding and meditation opportunities opening. I'm very clear this is happening only because of my working with Source. I am not responsible. I do my inner work and I show up but there is an easiness to the flow of my days that is not of my doing.

It took me so long to learn these truths! I really believed what I was taught when I was young. I tried to live according to "their" rules but it didn't work. Now I feel free but mostly blessed. In church at the end we say, "Wherever I am, God is." I feel that.

I like that I pay attention to my feelings and don't fear them. I learn from them. Even psychologists look down on embracing too much vulnerability. I had to get away from the professionals to be myself. It's really so simple. Just be myself, allow, and pay attention.

October 22

I feel great, think hopefully, and even walk straighter. For the depth of my positive intentions, I'm surprised I don't fly. Everything is working well — what I need appears and struggles are, essentially, eliminated. I love it.

And then there's my walking. Better but not great.

This afternoon I picked up **Choose Them Wisely** by Dooley and opened it randomly. I read:

Keep in mind that just because you can't see your dreams coming true doesn't mean they aren't. Remember this during lulls in your week, month, or year. Just because you are not consciously aware of the wonderful "accidents" and serendipitous "coincidences" that you're about to experience doesn't mean that these ducks aren't now being lined up! Even as you read this, in the cosmos that now surrounds you and holds you in the palm of its hand, things are happening in your favor.

October 23

I wrote the November newsletter today:

In September I spoke at Unity about loving unconditionally. When we love unconditionally, we don't pay attention to conditions. Instead, we focus on appreciating the Source essence of the one we view. Now, I'd like to consider our part in receiving unconditional love.

Each of us maintains a vibrational atmosphere. We are vibrational beings in a vibrational world. Our thoughts and beliefs affect the vibration we practice. You choose the beliefs you keep active. Some folks think that anything that has happened is truth. They hold onto that vibration and they keep it active. Many folks keep thoughts and beliefs active that don't serve them. You may say, "Well, this victimization happened. It's the truth so I believe it."

Don't let the "truth" of something be the determinant. Many, many things are true. Keep active the vibration of the things you want to replicate. You are a vibrational being and life responds to your vibration. Everything that you experience is because you have chosen a particular vibration, either deliberately or by default. Life doesn't happen randomly. The vibration you maintain is reflected in your finances, your clothes, your health, your relationships. Everything you notice is about you.

While we acknowledge that at our core we are Source, we seem to believe that in some ways we are separate from Source. Source never withholds from us, is always focused on us, constantly surrounds us with attention, appreciation, and unspeakable love. We're either allowing through choosing the path of least resistance or resisting through practicing guardedness. Focusing on things around you holds you in a vibration that keeps you from experiencing the love that is being flowed to you at all times.

What are you doing with your thoughts that is letting in or resisting this unconditional love? Are you creating conditions by your vibrational frequency that are not allowing unconditional love? In our daily life whatever happens — traffic, job opportunities, interpersonal experiences, encounters with strangers — responds to our vibrational atmosphere. You create purposefully or by default. If you let yourself respond to conditions around you, you are not allowing yourself to receive love unconditionally.

Decide to choose the vibrational atmosphere you consciously want to create rather than responding in a knee-jerk fashion to this condition and that condition and the other condition. Rather than looking outside of yourself for praise or appreciation to make you feel good about yourself, look for it where it really is — inside. Unconditional love and appreciation are always available from Source. If you are looking for it anywhere else, you're looking for love in all the wrong places. Every place is the wrong place to look for love if it's not inside, from Source.

By choosing to be happy, we practice the path of least resistance. We allow ourselves to be seen, to be known, to be adored with no condition, for no reason, without merit. We practice self-acceptance and allow Source who knows us best to love us. Source loves us more than we can imagine and always loves us unconditionally. Are you open to receiving unlimited unconditional love?

October 24

Receiving unconditional love. Apparently, this is my new challenge. That involves trust, good self-esteem, confidence, and an awareness of partnership with Source. No wonder most folks don't do it. But I will.

Integrating my vulnerability is a big part of receiving love. Vulnerability isn't neediness but I mistook the two in my young years. Needing anything or anyone signaled danger so I tried to minimize my needs. Vulnerability is absolutely required now. I'm seeing the need for my clients to acknowledge it, so I know I need to recognize it in me.

It doesn't scare me now. It's an easy flow and shift. It's flexible because it isn't based on need. I know my worth and I don't need approval. My partnership is strong and I completely trust it.

I'm vulnerable with my walking challenges. I want to integrate that vulnerability and practice availability. I feel anchored in each second and appreciative.

Two coincidences today tell me Source is with me. I saw a hummingbird alight on the tree limb outside my window. I don't know if I've ever seen a hummingbird still. Then I encountered my adversary at the mailboxes. I didn't recognize him so I walked up. He mentioned my improved walking. He offered conversation and I responded politely. I'm so relieved that this unfinished business is resolved. I have avoided him for years and knew I should get past it but couldn't on my own. Source provided the perfect condition.

Meditating with Ginny for 45-60 minutes before the noon meditation group adds such a wonderful dimension to my days.

Seems like I am receiving love.

October 26

Listening to Abraham yesterday I was struck by the comment, "It's so easy." Abraham responded to an attendee arguing for her limitations. For Source, everything is so easy. Healing my body and my feelings and any imbalance is so easy. All I need do is align myself with Source.

October 27

For years I've appreciated Rob Brezsny's horoscopes. He has a feel for unconscious dynamics and the opportunities for healing they present. I can usually apply his general words to my specific concerns in meaningful ways that structure my perceptions more clearly.

This month the same horoscope was printed every week:

The driest place on the planet is the Atacama Desert in northern Chile. It gets about a half-inch of rain per year. And yet in 2011, archaeologists discovered that it's also home to a site containing the fossilized skeletons of numerous whales and other ancient sea creatures. I'm detecting a metaphorically comparable anomaly in your vicinity. A seemingly arid, empty part of your life harbors buried secrets that are available for you to explore. If you follow the clues, you may discover rich pickings that will inspire you to revise your history.

Leona, the minister at church, spoke about self-forgiveness. When she suggested forgiving ourselves "for self-condemnation" something inside me rocked and creaked and I knew the message was for me. I've hated Controllers around me but the relentlessly abusive Inner Critic has been successful in intimidating me. However, that part is me. I have damaged myself. I have curtailed my own aliveness more than another person ever could. My bent over walking is like bowing in the face of life's challenges. I haven't acted strong or stood upright and I think it's because of me, my reverence for my Critic. I take her seriously when I should have backed off and observed her. I am so sorry I've hurt myself so much.

There's really no one to hate. I am my worst enemy and a dastardly adversary. (Another former adversary came up to me today and made a point of saying hello.) Time to make peace with adversaries, my Critic included. Especially my Critic.

October 31

I'm surprised and pleased when I recognize how well my days are going. I've meditated silently for an hour three days this week with Ginny before the guided meditation group at noon. Small difficulties have evaporated. Larger challenges resolve easily. I have more energy and finish tasks around the house. I've received two referrals from a new referral source. Sleep has been good. And yesterday my neighbor brought me a gift from Rouen, France, where she vacationed — chocolate dusted almonds which I have searched for since July. I didn't realize until later in the day that that was another (unspoken and unrecognized) request answered. I feel like the Universe is listening and is responding to my wants.

My walking feels more even and less labored. Improvement in that area is slow but definitely there. I am encouraged.

I'm more peaceful than I've ever felt. Getting away from the Controller orientation I was taught has opened life to me. Knowing Source is with me allows me to accept others who aren't.

November 4

I felt free today. So many years I didn't realize the binding from the shame. It wrapped around me like a boa constrictor circling my throat. It's a different world without the shame.

I saw a new client and received a referral from a new referral source.

The meditation group was good. We are getting smaller and more powerful. It's magic. As soon as we had started I received an insight in response to a question asked of me just before the group. Magic. I feel so connected and, consequently, so worthy.

I am very pleased that I have more energy. Most days I rest once instead of twice. I like being a little more active and I really like my body straightening itself. Tension has been released.

I'm waiting for inspiration to tell me when to leave the house in the mornings to go to the gym. Each time I do, I enter the gym and immediately have a lane in the pool awaiting me. A watchful presence protects and guides me. I love how it has come about through focus and trust in this second and not from focusing on the past. What needs to be healed comes up and is healed. I don't do anything. My job is to be aware and allowing.

November 5

Today I'm receiving miracles. I'm standing straighter and walking more easily. Several days ago I had requested a nice interaction at the gym. Today a swimming friend complimented me on my improved stroke. She's the only person in the world who is aware of how I swim and open to comment. It was very kind of her; my heart is touched. I feel blessed that the Universe is working to support me.

Another Universal intervention — I had been asking for guidance about a local in-person continuing education class of 3-4 hours. At the dentist's office yesterday, the dentist handed me a brochure for CE seminars and then last night he called and left a message about more CE opportunities! What a surprise. I didn't expect CE information to come from my dentist! It feels like a Universal intervention. These specific classes may not work but I feel heard and acknowledged.

My body feels relaxed. My creativity flows. I see a new opening and the possibility of joy and expansion.

November 7

Constrictions from fear make me mad. I don't have any more time to hide. My alignment with Source is enough to trust. I don't need approval from anyone. I'm putting my work out there because this is my life's contribution. This is who I am and I am good enough.

November 9

In meditation yesterday I saw myself walking very well. At lunch with Jan we talked and laughed and cried. I came back and walked better and farther than I have in a while. Maybe laughing has something to do with healing?

November 10

Yesterday a new woman came to the meditation group. She was identified with her Controller, not offensively but enough for me to notice. I felt heavy this morning. Why should her being in her Controller bother me? Clearly, it is not about her personally. When I stay in my Adult, I can accept her choice to live any way she chooses.

But another, being in her Controller, throws me into my powerless, resentful Child. Why should that be? I lose my boundaries and my sense of being able to control my event. She requested at the end of the group that we introduce ourselves (again). Really quite assertive for a first time attendee but OK.

So, I gather she is an Enneagram 1, my mother's type. But why the anger? Because I need to forgive at a deeper level. I sincerely want to do that. At this point my (four years deceased) mother is available to me; I can feel that. She is 100% healed and happy and loving and giving and protective. I didn't get what I wanted from her when I was young but I did learn so much that benefits me now. She did the best she could. And I am not doing the best I can if I hold onto the powerless and resentful past. I will never be healthy, physically or emotionally, until I am unswervingly anchored in my Adult.

So, it's my Controller! The new woman was showing me myself. How humbling!!!! In the meditation today we released the past and closed the door. I'm locking mine. I've had enough of it! Only joy and presence and creativity for me now.

November 11

I feel happy, excited, supported, and motivated. If the Universe invites, I am available!

November 12

I'm visualizing myself walking perfectly. I'm confident and optimistic. I'm relieved to be free of the past. And tomorrow I will actually go to the park and walk the quarter mile circuit.

The talk with Jason lets me know that I want to walk perfectly in six weeks when I send him the manuscript. Sooner than I had planned but no problem. When I'm in the field, I'm unlimited. I didn't know life could be so rewarding.

November 13

Today before meditation Carolyn spoke about her health concerns. Plaque is building in her arteries and it's not from her eating. She stated that she will slow down, looking defeated while saying it. We focused on health in the meditation. The intuitive sense I had was that slowing down will release resistance and allow her to receive from the Universe. Slowing down is not the beginning of the end but finding a new track with rewards the mind doesn't understand. A good message for me, too.

November 15

No one came to meditation today! That tells me I'm entering a new phase. When I meditated what I received was that the work has been done; wait for the manifestations. What a lovely message.

I do feel relaxed and trusting and more intuitive than ever. I have such a strong, clear sense of Source presence.

I didn't know life could be so good. And so easy.

November 16

Oprah Winfrey's name came to mind yesterday. I decided to buy some new slippers. That's what I wear in the house and my old ones were inching out of the acceptable category. I found three pairs I appreciated so I bought all three! How completely indulgent. But that's what Oprah would do. I feel prosperous.

Looking over my client schedule for this week, I notice I have a client scheduled every day after meditation. That was something I've wanted but haven't formalized as a request, just a thought. I'm receiving what I think about.

At the park yesterday and today, I've walked the whole circuit. I had guessed it to be 1/4 mile but heard today it's 1.2 miles! Granted, yesterday I stopped twice and today three times briefly. (My

Controller is quick to remind me of my limitations, bless her heart.) But I'm reassured and expecting walking to get easier. I can see my dream materializing.

I feel happy and optimistic and at home in my life. Having a clear, working relationship with Source comforts me more than anything.

November 17

My gifts fell over each other today. Having walked a mile on Sat. and on Sun., I wanted to walk a mile this morning. But I received another gift — two new clients. I scheduled one this morning and one this afternoon, before and after meditation. They are both lovely women, good referrals. It's fun to have many referrals but the truth is most of them are very short-term and uninterested in working at some depth. These two women, however, are reflective, intelligent, and suffering from their Controller's will. The Enneagram serves me well in knowing folk's psychodynamic challenges quickly. One is a 1, needing to integrate her vulnerability. The other seems to be a 6, needing to trust herself.

I'm so grateful that my professional life is gratifying. I love my work and I can't imagine anything better. I love private practice. I love seeing clients in their homes or at Unity in the meeting room. I love setting my own schedule, doing therapy the way that fits for me, and even doing my own billing.

And I noticed that some tightness has relaxed in my hips so I am walking more evenly easily. I'm standing straighter. The first limit at the beginning of menopause 9.5 years ago was not being able to tuck my hips under and stand straight. Now that seems to be reversing without my attention. What an incredible gift. I couldn't do it on my own but now it happens without my attention.

Only to myself had I thought that starting to swim earlier would be fun. I needed to interrupt my swim to go to the bathroom today and in that five minutes I encountered another swimmer who swims earlier than I do. She told me that she's not swimming tomorrow and offered me her lane earlier !! That never happens but it happened for me at exactly the minute I could take advantage of it. Source is so with me.

November 18

Of the several gifts today, one stands out. I had reserved the office at Unity but it was busy when my client was scheduled. I stood in the hallway and thought. While I was there, the Montessori director walked by. We hadn't connected in months and she was receptive. She also let me use her office at exactly the minute I needed it. As my client entered, she, graciously, left.

I've noticed about Source that timing is everything. It's not about the future or the past but being available in the present second.

November 19

I felt a gentle squeeze from the Universe last night. Jon Stewart interviewed a colleague of Edward Snowden's. "Was he naive?" Jon asked. She looked away for a second and said, "He is idealistic."

I twinge at the word naive. When I worked at the prison doing groups for the mentally ill inmates, my supervisor told me that the other psychologists had spoken about me and called me naive. Then she laughed. That destroyed my peace about being at the prison and left me bruised.

I am idealistic and I was then. I wanted to offer the men something they could use and I sincerely wanted to make a difference. The state employees generally didn't respond well to me. I didn't fit in (as 4s are wont to say) but hearing (and fantasizing) that I was dissed by a professional group cut me. I continued to do the best job I could but with no illusion that I was respected by my peers.

Hearing the hurting word "naive" coupled with the inspirational word "idealistic" healed that old sadness for me. It wasn't anything I was thinking about or even aware of but the Universe delivered a gift to me.

It's easy to forgive when I'm so loved by the Universe. I can release that memory entirely now.

A healing came for me. I didn't know I needed it and did nothing to effect it but I recognized it immediately and I'm certainly grateful. How can I not feel special when the Universe takes such precisely perfect care of me?

November 20

I wrote the December newsletter today.

From: **Rewire and Evolve your Brain** by Joe Dispenza (paraphrased)

Did you create your day this morning? Did you wake up, excited about creating your day, applying your wisdom and your insights to your life?

If life is routine and predictable, we haven't mastered observation. We need to pay attention really well. Paying attention and concentration are skills that improve with practice. When we meditate we don't respond to the environment, to our bodies, or to time. We move into the quantam field. When form is separate from consciousness, we can experience spontaneous healing.

Folks who become healthy "all of a sudden" have in common:

1. They accepted and believed that there is an Intelligence living within them that is giving them life. "I'm connected to a Force greater than me that loves me more than I love myself. If I can make contact with this Intelligence, it will be healing for me." They believe that it's like riding on the back of a giant and whispering in its ear, that that intelligence holds order for everything in the Universe. They believe that they are connected to it, that something loves them enough to give them life. They choose to surrender to that force and get out of the way.

2. They believe that their thoughts created their condition. If they believed they were victims or angry persons, that thought affected their health. Dispenza notes that every thought creates a chemical. The chemicals your body creates make you feel the way you're thinking. That state then creates more chemicals which elicit more of the same feelings. Your thinking derives from your feeling. So, how you perceive reality depends upon your feelings.

3. The healthy folks said, "I have to reinvent myself. I can't be a miserable victim the rest of my life. I have to be somebody else. What would it be like to be a happy person? What would I have to change about myself to live in joy?" To reassemble their brains to produce a new way of being, they chose to contemplate a new future. Their brains started to organize themselves in a new way, changing their thinking. Learning is making new neurological connections. They grew new circuits just by thinking/rehearsing/visualizing. Memory is repetition to reinforce a new idea. Sustainable

circuits act as platforms for who the creators will become, rehearsing who they will be.

4. They became so involved in what they were doing they lost track of time, the body, and the environment. That's when they walk through the door to the quantam field. The frontal lobe is most active, the orchestra leader. It quiets the association centers, the motor centers, and the emotional centers. When we make new circuits, we perceive what already existed but we never really saw. We perceive the world differently and process our experience differently.

November 23

I spoke at Unity today, having heard at 6:30 last night that Leona is unavailable. I wanted to go into it without anxiety or pressure. I made notes, organized a stream of thoughts, and focused for 30 minutes. Then I relaxed and trusted that it would be fine.

It was fine. We had more music than usual and another congregation member wanted to share her presentation. I didn't have time for my talk but I did lead a guided meditation about practicing gratitude for the reality we are creating which has not manifest yet. Two people spoke to me afterward, thanking me.

My goal of staying relaxed was met. The service was fine but funky. The noon meditation here afterward was good with two participants. I'm moving into the next stage — competent professional who is self-accepting and accepted by others. It feels a little strange but my goal is to always be trusting and surrendered. I need to not think any more. Just allow.

November 24

I'm surprised at how happy I am. Everything seems to unfold smoothly. I receive gifts. When I leave the front door open, flies stay out. Source seems so close. I feel comforted and confirmed.

My walking improves. I'm not where I want to be but I can tell I'm on track to get there. I'm beyond confident. I know my perfect walking continues to manifest more and more clearly. I feel a quiet, pervasive joy I've not felt before. I'm aware of feeling at home on this planet, also something I've never felt. I'm not afraid of others and not doubting myself. And it's because I'm letting Source work through me. My reliance is complete.

November 26

Don't take anything personally.

Don't make any issue interpersonal.

November 27

It's Thanksgiving and I am so thankful. I walked two miles this morning. It wasn't pretty and it wasn't fast but I did it and I know I will continue to do it. That's been my goal — walking two miles. It isn't the end point but it does shatter a limiting ceiling.

What will limit me? Not the diagnosis or my past or my old beliefs. I feel empowered and supported and overwhelmingly optimistic. I know my life will improve in ways I can't foresee. I am grateful.

PART TWO

PSYCHOLOGY
MEDITATION
SPIRITUALITY

Psychology

We heal our wounds and practice good mental health in our daily choices. That firm psychological foundation underlies a mature spirituality. Some considerations about working with our inner worlds follow.

Darkness and Brilliance

Darkness scares us. Darkness around us leads us to move cautiously. Darkness inside us hides the brilliance at our core.

Internal darkness offers us an opportunity for self-discovery. We have been taught that, theoretically, we contain everything. All facets of life are ours to experience. What we don't want to know gets pushed into the darkness. It breaks through in dreams or slips of the tongue or projection.

Integrating the brilliance at our center is our life's work. We need to move through the internal rubble created by our refusal to own different aspects of ourselves. Only then can we know the outside situation as it is and not as we are. Until we do our work, our perceptions distort and confuse our inner and outer worlds. We see outside what we refuse to see inside and then draw conclusions about the world. When we won't accept our feelings, we get stuck in our intellects and trust them to do a job they were never meant to do—finding meaning in our experience.

In the second half of life we are challenged to integrate those parts of ourselves hidden by the darkness. They are not evil, although we have distrusted them. We have chosen a façade to hide behind instead of embracing the darkness. By avoiding honesty, we have quashed our brilliance. Healing requires surrender. When we finally acknowledge that our thinking doesn't make life work, we move into another realm. We observe, we allow, we experience, and we trust the healing process. Now we choose presence and immediacy and trust. We practice availability in the moment. We will endure anything to move fully into our aliveness.

A peace we did not manufacture lives at our center. We can only get there by moving through all the feelings stirred up by our life experiences. When we live from the peace in our center we cooperate with Life in the ever-creative flow of becoming. That is when we own our power. It moves through us and emanates from us. We open receptively to Life, knowing that all is well. In this creative process we allow ourselves to be carried and we always say, "Yes."

Don't Be So Sensitive

Have you ever heard those words? I have, a million times, and I tried to accede to them for decades. I thought my sensitivity was preventing me from fitting in and I wanted to be "normal."

I couldn't do it, no matter how much I tried. When I pretended to be what I thought was acceptable, I looked foolish. I knew that I couldn't let myself be known for who I really was so I had to develop diversionary techniques. I learned to listen and ask questions and keep the spotlight off me. The ersatz relationships which evolved weren't satisfying but I thought that at some point I would feel safe enough to open up. Not so.

I spent a lot of time alone. I worked very hard on myself to correct some deep error that had been made in my creation. I thought that with enough effort I could earn entry into The Group but the more I meditated, journalled, and experienced my feelings, the less I could share with most folks and the harder it became to find any meaningful common ground. I had effectively dug myself into a (w)hole. And since I couldn't escape myself, I learned attention and presence and how to listen to the still, small voice within. I acknowledge that this was my default position which I embraced only after nothing else offered respite from the pain of being human and lonely.

Now in mid-life I am grateful that I didn't receive what I thought I wanted. If I had fit in, I would have lost myself. All those hours alone taught me to look at how I had learned to hate myself, taking my cues from others who hated their vulnerability. I wanted to be liked by people who didn't like themselves. They taught me to look OK and always to say "Fine" when asked how I was and that pretending would suffice.

But since I'm not normal, I couldn't do it. I didn't feel OK and I didn't want to say "Fine" and I couldn't pretend. I was too sensitive. And after all those years alone with my sensitivity, I learned to love it! I can meditate now and reach a peace and wisdom that can't be given, precisely because of my sensitivity. I can feel another person's pain and know what it's like to be her and, in that way, heal us both. Only because of my sensitivity. I can hear with my heart, not just with my head, and experience Life, not just talk about it. Again, due to my sensitivity which I realize is one of my finest qualities.

I have worked hard to hone my sensitivity, to know it, and now to trust it. It's what makes sense of Life. Because of my sensitivity I can appreciate how what the stranger said to me reveals my own buried feelings. I've learned to notice the outside reflecting the inside. It's my sensitivity that lets me see patterns in my interactions and then to understand that Life is opening a new window to knowing myself at a deeper level. Sensitivity allows me to form a partnership with Life and to know that I'm not alone on a profound level. And that makes everything worthwhile.

I'm glad I'm too sensitive!

Embracing Vulnerability

Throughout our lives we learn how to manage our feelings, demand respect, influence others, speak convincingly, carry ourselves with dignity, and hold our boundaries. We can impress and sometimes intimidate and once in a while challenge. We know how to move through the outer world. But when is it time to move into those soft spots inside and say, "I embrace you and I love you"?

Why do that? Isn't vulnerability what we want to erase? We hide our vulnerability from everyone else and we hide it from ourselves as long as we can. But, inevitably, there comes a point when we can't ignore the sleeplessness or the longing or the restlessness or the frustration. We can't keep pushing our way forward. And we don't want to. It has cost us too much.

By mid-life we don't even want to see our vulnerability as a problem. It's our core, the most basic part of who we are. How could that be a problem?! We want to say "Yes" to every aspect of ourselves because this is who we are! And we want to shout our affirmation of ourselves. "Yes, this is me! Yes, I'm hurting. Yes, I cry. Yes."

And in our "Yes" we find peace. It's not our job to try, to effort, or to wear ourselves out. It's our job to be ourselves, whatever that means. We're not trying to be good enough or lovable. We don't need approval. We need to be alive and to feel ourselves and be. Just be. We've done enough.

Embracing our vulnerability, we cooperate with Life. We allow ourselves to be as we are and we allow Life to guide us. We don't need the Controller in our minds to tell us what is appropriate. By owning the deepest parts of ourselves, we find freedom and passion and creativity. What joy!

Gratitude

Sometimes it seems we're blocked on all sides. No matter what we choose or what we do, we can't move ourselves out of a stuck position. Those are the times to sit back, breathe, and practice gratitude.

I am grateful for the very smallest of blessings. I'm glad I have fingernails. What would life be like without them? I don't even want to imagine. I'm grateful I have toes. I appreciate that I can smell and taste even if the smells and tastes aren't always pleasant.

When I adopt an attitude of gratitude, my relationship to Life shifts. I'm not trying to be in control or to work my will. I'm not resentful because I don't focus on what I don't like. I am humble. I realize that this minute will pass soon enough and I don't resist anything. When I cooperate with what is presented to me, I relax.

Being grateful is the best way I know to cooperate with Life. I don't erect any barriers through my judgments about what should be. I don't even think about "should." I just say, "Yes" and "Thank you."

I find this practice especially helpful with feelings which scare me or challenge me. I don't like feeling angry but sometimes I am. Instead of pretending I'm not or rationalizing and thinking, I accept my anger. I say, "Yes and thank you," and I breathe. I know it's OK to be angry and I also know I use good judgment about choosing appropriate behavior.

When someone says something which wounds, I respond with "Thank you." I don't want to take offense and barricade my heart. I want to learn from the situation. Being grateful helps me stay open to receive. And for whatever I receive, I say, "Thank you." Not to anyone in particular. Just to Life. "Thank you, Life, for giving me whatever the day brings."

Moving through life gratefully reduces stress, promotes better physical and mental health, and improves relationships. We feel happier and we think more clearly. And that's a lot to be grateful for!

Freedom in the Pen

When new attendees enter stress management, anger management, or depression management, we breathe. I facilitate groups for mentally ill inmates at a men's state penitentiary. The group members have been diagnosed as having a thought disorder or a feeling disorder. They may have a short prison term or a life term. Most have substance abuse in their backgrounds. Today they cope with incarceration and its stresses. They can't walk 100 yards in a straight line and some never will again. They eat what is given to them, not what they want. Privacy is lacking and quiet comes only in the early morning hours.

At the first class I talk about attention and I guide them through a breathing exercise in which we focus on the in-breaths and the out-breaths. We look at the breath. We don't criticize the breath or change the breath. We simply practice focusing our attention and the breath is always available so we focus on that. We don't mention the word meditation and we don't intellectualize. We only experience.

I tell them that we are not trying to achieve anything by breathing; we just practice presence in each second. Anything that occurs around us is acceptable. They learn not to be concerned with what isn't their business. The difference between what they can control and what they cannot control becomes clear.

At the end of class I say that the second daily practice in addition to being Observers inside is to be Observers outside. We don't take anything personally. No matter what anyone does or says, it's not personal to us. It's personal to the speaker and we don't have to react. Being in their detached Observer gives them time and space so they don't get caught up in another inmate's drama.

At the next few classes we talk about forgiveness. They say it's easier to forgive others than to forgive themselves. They carry significant self-hate and admit that they deserve incarceration even though they suffer. Keeping their hearts closed promised them safety in a cruel world. Now, opening those bruised and wounded hearts challenges the inmates.

I encourage them to be their own best friend. I suggest that they pat themselves on the back each night for doing something right that day. Relating to themselves as responsible adults fosters a sense of integrity. They learn to refer to themselves for judgment about how they live.

We practice gratitude. Many say they are grateful to wake up each day. I encourage them to give thanks for small things—having fingernails, being able to tie their shoes, and having a bed. (It's a relief for many of the mentally ill not to be homeless.) And then I recommend being grateful for what they don't like and don't want—saying thank you to themselves for the cell mate who snores, accepting rude words from an officer without responding and blessing him silently, being grateful when no mail arrives. They learn that their circumstances don't determine their behavior or their feelings.

After weeks of practice I notice that the committed men are stiller, apparently more at peace with themselves, more present to the moment with less talk about the future. They are more available to their brothers who need guidance. I'm touched by their patience with the inmate who is developmentally delayed or by their explanation (in street terms) of why we breathe. ("It's so we don't hit the guy who pisses us off. I used to just cut anyone who dissed me but now I can wait and see that he's just a loser who ain't doing too good himself.")

Their words are crude but the longer they breathe and practice being in their Observers the more I can feel their gentleness, the part of themselves they tried to destroy decades ago. They remain basically decent humans struggling to climb through layers and layers of hate and guilt and confusion. They gave up on themselves when everyone else gave up on them. They didn't know how they were going to survive the pain and alienation and solitude of their miserable lives.

By breathing and identifying with their Observers, they find a meaning to their existence which they haven't known. They can't articulate a philosophy but they wake up each day with some small hope and some willingness to reach out. They don't necessarily understand why their outlook has changed but without thought they replace their previous addictive behavior with their new-found commitment to breathing and observing.

They find power inside themselves instead of by using their fists. Their journey all along has been one of Warrior but now they see it's a Spiritual Warrior with their own demons not with others. In the past it was easier to focus on another man than to face their inner turmoil. With their skills of detached observing and breathing they can process any feeling or thought or impulse without destructive action.

They say they feel freer practicing breathing and detached observing in prison than they ever felt on the streets. They had imprisoned themselves in their minds years ago when they tried to escape from themselves. Now when they open to every part of themselves, they resist nothing and resent nothing and accept what exists each second. They say they have found freedom.

How do You Imprison Yourself?

We'd all like to say "Oh, no, I don't do that." But the truth is we do. We all do and usually we don't know we're severely limiting ourselves.

Maybe you think, "I can't achieve that." Or "I'll never have what I want. It's just not possible for me." Or "Life's not fair and I've been dealt a truly terrible hand."

Excuses abound. It's easier to point to something or someone outside us as the cause of our misery but it's never NEVER the truth. Children are victims but if you are over the age of fourteen, I want to know how you think and how you cut off your feelings and what you believe. You are your worst enemy.

What is your belief about receiving love or money or success or acclaim or friendship or justice?

What is your belief about your own worthiness? What about losing what you want?

What is your belief about trusting Life?

How do you hate yourself? Procrastination? Overdoing anything—eating, drinking, gambling, working, exercise, TV viewing, talking? What is your addiction—your favorite way to avoid feeling?

How To Respond

We don't choose (consciously) what happens to us but we always have a choice about how we respond. We each have many aspects to our being. And each of those aspects offers us a way of perceiving and thinking and responding.

I call our many parts subpersonalities. We each have an Adult who thinks rationally and can be objective, a Child filled with feelings, a Controller who shields us from vulnerability, a Rebellious Teenager who will not acquiesce, a Nurturing Parent who supports our Child in her growth, a Spiritual Seeker who envisions a greater reality than can be seen by the eyes, a Victim who whines, and many more. Some of us have a well-defined Artist. Others have an Athlete. These subpersonalities are normal and healthy and enrich our lives.

When it comes to responding to circumstances, we want to choose which subpersonality will decide and act responsibly. Our Child may instantaneously know how she feels and what she wants but our Adult may prefer a steadier, reasoned way of responding. No one subpersonality should dominate exclusively. In business perhaps we defer to our Business Person with her choice to remain unemotional. In affairs of the heart we may lead with our feelings.

But choosing who inside of us will respond demands a conscious decision. Are we aware of our Powerless Child and how her frustration and consequent anger lead her to view the world as threatening? With that Powerless Child's assumptions about life—"I won't be heard, I won't be trusted, I won't be respected"—of course her response is angry. She is unable to connect with an adult, to form a working partnership, or to delay reacting. Her response is designed to relieve her tension in the moment. And that's all.

In contrast, our Mature Adult knows that we each have needs and differences. Our Adult respects those differences and treats others the way she wants to be treated. She knows that when she is hurt, the other person probably doesn't understand what she did or perhaps is also hurting herself. She knows that we are all in this to grow and to heal. She is patient with others and with herself.

Our Spiritual Seeker knows that a greater reality encompasses us all. She sees that our interactions seem designed to promote healing for everyone even when the interactions are unpleasant. She doesn't take anything personally because she knows that it is only by having experiences that we learn and grow. Whatever happens she says, "So be it." And she moves on and asks for whatever is next. She is open and humble and grateful.

We always have a choice. From which part of you do you want to respond today?

Healing

When we take experience as our basis for living, we value everything that happens. No matter what it is, we look at it, feel the feelings associated with it, notice how it fits the long-term patterns in our lives, and say, "What am I to learn from this experience?" There is no good and no bad, just *what is*. After an unpleasant encounter, I say, "What am I being shown about myself?" Everything becomes an opportunity to learn and to grow.

Soon we see consistencies and we notice that what happens around us reflects what happens within us. If I'm critical of myself, I'll find others who criticize me. If I'm insensitive to my Child's needs, I'll find others who will not treat my needs sensitively. I learn that reality inside and outside is seamless.

We all have healing work to be done psychologically. Perhaps it's healing a fear or a co-dependency that hides vulnerability or an addiction that masks rage. Whatever our challenge this lifetime, we are given opportunities to work through our defenses and then our wounds. Life presents these opportunities perfectly. Our minds don't understand, but we acknowledge that they are not important in our healing anyway. We learn to trust Life more than our minds and to say "Yes" to what comes because we know an intelligence greater than ours is choreographing our healing for us.

Life is for healing. And Life will show us how to go about healing in a way that is precise for each of us. We experience what we don't expect and often don't want and, by not resisting Life, we heal. We form an alliance with Life and cooperate with the forces that move and shape our days. Thus, we practice non-resistance.

Healing requires trust and surrender and a willingness to experience everything. This openness to experience frightens but strengthens.

We pass through feelings which shake our deepest roots and we live through it. The next time we're not as afraid because we've been here before. Feelings are just feelings—important to acknowledge, important not to resist, and important not to get stuck in.

We learn that we're just "moving through" on this journey with nothing to attach to. Everything is a lesson. One step in healing and owning our power is letting go and allowing. We accept whatever life brings and we look deeper. Always we say "Yes." We don't have to understand but we do have to cooperate with Life in our healing.

At mid-life the unconscious becomes more active than it has been since childhood. This is when we truly leave the driving to Someone Else and tolerate the ride. By the end of mid-life we know ourselves differently, we may live somewhere new, and our work may be different. We have surrendered and let Life lead us. Because we have learned to cooperate with Life and to trust its guidance, the changes are an exciting part of the adventure.

Mid-Life Psychology

In our 20's and 30's we worked to develop competence in the world. We wanted to establish a place for ourselves. Our inner worlds may have been a bit fuzzy and incomprehensible but we focused on polishing our outer world facades and that was sufficient.

But now in our 40's and 50's, it's no longer enough. We have achieved some measure of success but, strangely, we're dissatisfied and we can't explain why. Nothing is wrong exactly, but nothing is right enough. We must have MORE and we must have it NOW. Something is gnawing at our souls and no matter what we "do" we can't assuage the restlessness.

Slowly it dawns on us that it isn't a matter of "doing" at all. It's time to "be" in a different way and we can't willfully manufacture that. By our mid to late 40's life has confronted us with the truth about who we truly are. Those demons that have been living in the shadows inside roar and demand that we acknowledge them now. We <u>must</u> feel the hurt from the childhood loneliness which we've pushed away with our life-of-the-party act. We can't escape the anger that still smolders. That seemingly bottomless pit of need and want waits for us and will not be covered over. Now is the time and our inner world is the place. Healing is finally possible.

Surrender is the key mid-life term. Through surrender—feeling whatever feelings come and accepting whatever situations arise—we find resolution. Our lifelong conflicts seem to melt away as we release our resistance. Finally, we are on top of our lives and not because of our efforts but because we have relinquished efforting.

The surrender we experience in mid-life opens us to partnership. This process of integration that occurs (without our conscious assent) is a basically spiritual one. We reunite with parts of ourselves we have distrusted or feared and disowned and through this integration we find peace. We realize a creativity and an aliveness that we have not before known. We see opportunities that had been hidden when we relied upon our logic.

It happens only through surrender and only at mid-life. From that point on, this partnership with the larger whole which we have established through listening to our inner worlds guides our days. We find that we are not alone.

Attention in Mid-Life

By mid-life the rules have changed. No longer are our days about striving, focusing on achieving a goal, or keeping someone comfortable. Now our attention goes to realms inside we haven't visited. We explore our own undeveloped capacities. Never played duplicate bridge? Let's do it now. Never danced onstage? Now is the time. We pick up the paint brush or the camera or the backpack or the pen and we allow our creativity to guide us.

"Allow" and "creativity" are mid-life words. They connote our respect for our partnership with Life and our trust that what we don't understand knows what's best for us. We move enthusiastically into spaces we've never travelled.

We explore the depths behind our feelings. Maybe we've always been caught by our neediness. Now we don't let our fear stop us. Trying to satisfy those needs has never worked anyway—not with love or food or drink or money or prestige. Those same old feelings of "I want," "I need," "I long for" still exist but now we move into our Observer and we say, "OK, tell me about it." And we sit still and pay complete attention to those feelings and we don't do anything. That's right. We don't solve our "problems" for we see that our so-called "problem" is a beautiful, valuable part of who we are. We want to know that part of yourself and help it develop and mature and blossom. There is always a gift hidden by the pain and now we demand the gift!

Creativity doesn't come from our head or from our training or from anything external. Creativity is the experience of allowing Life to guide us and following with humility and attention and commitment. And always saying "Yes." We are all artists with our consciousness and in mid-life our consciousness expands. We release limitations and identify with our source, not our intellect. We open to anything. Finally, we're ready. We know that who we are is valuable and that we must offer our gifts to the world. So we do, because we must.

Freedom

The bonds from our unresolved inner conflicts restrict us far more than limitations from any situation or physical handicap or financial lack. Our fears about our unlovableness may have (unconsciously) led us to construct defenses against intimacy. Our attempts to appear intellectual we hope impress others. We realize they don't quite obliterate the vulnerability that bubbles in the depth of our hearts but maybe no one will notice. We really don't want that insecurity seen. Not intimacy! No, just look at the parts of me which my mind likes—my wit, my figure, my snappy repartee. And that's all I will look at, also. We pretend the sea of shadowy roiling lurching feelings doesn't really exist or isn't really so bad or is really a thyroid problem. Certainly, work and TV and drinking and socializing distract us. After all, everyone has something to complain about, right? Life's not perfect for anyone so we stop our grousing and act "practical" and grown up and try to fit in.

But at such a price. The Controller we have developed to silence our inner world woes also limits our aliveness and spontaneity and creativity and pretty soon we say, "I'm going through the motions and I look appropriate but I don't feel completely alive." And we're not. Grabbing that aliveness means committing to complete intimacy inside—being willing to feel every tiny little insignificant decades-old wince. Being as passive as the sand on the shore when the waves of hurt or anger or fear wash over us. And freedom is not fighting them, not judging them, not trying to control, not evaluating, not even reacting. It's freedom to say "Yes, thank you. I accept this moment."

The Controller whom we constructed to keep us safe has instead kept us dead. And mid-life is the time to embrace life and to experience. Anything at all, really, just experience it deeply and loudly and celebrate the opportunity to experience. Feeling anything at all has come to be such a gift. And when we attend to our feelings—watching them and experiencing them—we don't act them out. We have funded such a reserve of strength inside ourselves that we use our best judgment about healing our wounds by being good Parents to ourselves. Holding our hurt Child, not silencing her. Giving her the care she needs so she doesn't look to others or to addictions. We practice presence to ourselves deeply and compassionately and wisely.

In mid-life we can be unwavering in our presence to our inner worlds. We are available and attentive and we are not attached to outcomes. We relinquish all restricting controls and we say, "I am here." We are free because anything that happens, anything at all, is OK. We practice acceptance and our practice is more important that what it is we are accepting. Our freedom is internal. We are free to just be. And that's enough.

To Choose Happiness

The inmates I work with at the state penitentiary have very few choices. The young guys complain about being told what to do or being treated inconsiderately or losing privileges while the old timers just smile. They know those things carry no weight. They've taught me that one basic choice no one can take is their ability to choose happiness.

They know that happiness isn't a result of doing what you want or receiving what you request or being in control. Happiness is a response to life. It doesn't matter what the day's events may be, you can always choose happiness.

In that sense happiness isn't a feeling but a life stance. Happiness doesn't result from an occurrence over which we have no influence or even after a self-defined "victory." Happiness is a way of being. Happiness is saying "Yes" to life and "Thank you" and "I accept everything." Happiness is releasing resistance and overlooking our petty willfulness and choosing to be open-hearted. Happiness is living as large as we can and saying, "I'm so lucky to participate in this experience!" Happiness doesn't depend on feeling good or on things going right. We choose happiness because it's the wisest and most life-affirming choice we can make, not because it's logical.

Have you ever said, "If only I had more money or a great career or a super lover or (fill in the blank), then I'd be happy"? It actually works the other way around. When you are happy, then you receive gifts from the world. You bless Life and Life blesses you. But by then you will also realize that experiencing the magic and mystery of each moment is a greater gift than anything our minds concoct. Choosing happiness is choosing aliveness this moment, no matter how it feels. Funny, isn't it, that we work so hard to be happy when the opposite— surrender—is what's required?

The act of choosing happiness is a lesson in surrender and trust. A deep peace ensues and we know that by aligning with Life, we become more ourselves. It is proclaiming YES to life, not trying to manipulate or control. Happiness this way isn't fleeting. Since it doesn't depend on anything happening or not happening, just on our affirmation that we choose happiness, we're not in danger of losing it. We're completely "in control."

Trying to control our surroundings in order to feel happy is a doomed effort. Maybe that's why the inmates learn this lesson faster than the rest of us. Since they have no control and no hope of control, their choice is clear. The rest of us can learn from them.

Self-Induced Stress

Do you create stress for yourself?

We stress ourselves with our thinking, our unexamined habits, and our denial. Self-defeating thinking includes assumptions we have made about ourselves and the world which we don't recognize. Do you find yourself resenting others? Does it seem that life is easier for everyone else? Does anger pop up quickly? Do you speak when you wish you hadn't? Or don't speak and you wish you had? Do you feel like a Victim? Or a Bully?

You can change any scenario entirely on your own. Our consciousness is the basis for everything that happens in our lives. If you want to know what exists in your inner world, look around you. Is your mate abusive or insensitive? It's no coincidence. Something in you refuses to acknowledge your own needs and worth. He's just a mirror. Is your boss critical and humiliating? What in you is she reflecting? An abusive Inner Critic? The outside reflects the inside unerringly.

Having these mirrors makes our job of personal growth so much easier! We always assume that *what is* exists to help us. Nothing is a mistake. Circumstances seem to align to allow us the experience we need. "No," I can hear you protest, "I don't want to be humiliated and frustrated and disappointed." It's painful and maybe unfair, but for some reason you need that experience. We learn to focus on our experience and not the objective facts.

An appropriate and growthful response no matter what occurs is "Thank you." Whether we like what happens or not is irrelevant. If we accept *what is* with gratitude and release our resistance, we learn. Life knows better than our minds what we need in order to heal and grow. When we say "Thank you" we cooperate with life. Stress results from resisting the lessons life presents to us.

Inmates

What is around us reflects what is inside us. Working in a men's prison, I reflect on the experience of being incarcerated. The men can't walk too far in one direction, can't stand in groups on the yard, can't watch cable television or research the internet or visit a museum. What they can't do outnumbers what they can do by about 1000 to 1.

So many of them say they are angry about being in prison but they also admit they were angry before they entered prison. They say it angers them that they can't work for pay but admit they didn't show up for work when they lived "on the streets" before their jail time. They say that when they are released they will be happy but admit that they never have been happy. No matter what external changes they crave, their inner worlds seem locked up. Locked up by the anger they first felt when they were powerless children who were mercilessly abused. Locked up by their fear of yet another failure when they attempt to read or learn a trade or complete high school. Locked up by their inability to tolerate their own vulnerability which leads to rigidity, unconsciousness, and violent behavior.

These inmates are afraid of being present to themselves. They are afraid of feeling their longing and their hurt and their sadness. They choose hopelessness as a mask to forestall disappointment. The resulting numbness in their hearts can be tolerated.

Is that so different from how many of us middle class folks live? We're caught on the success treadmill and fear falling off the conveyor belt. We want to function as well as "everyone else" so we don't know what to do with our desperation and our emotional isolation. Maybe we can pretend these feelings are not there and then they won't be. We're willing to sacrifice some hope for security. Maybe we'll never try to paint or to sail or to live in Fiji or to hike through the West.

Our dreams seem expendable. We even feel good about choosing practicality.

But what have we lost? Inmates see the walls which limit them. The rest of us can't discern why we feel frustrated and restless and dissatisfied. Passion seems a luxury.

But by our 50's life demands that we embrace our passion and say "Yes" to what we don't understand and can't see. An invisible level of reality tugs incessantly until we deny it at the risk of losing our souls. It's a solitary jump by definition. Our focus shifts from outer world and intellectual concerns (a career, mortgage, family) to our shadowy inner world. No one else knows what it's like inside us. We're surprised by our sudden intolerance of what has always been OK. We must have more and we must have it now. We may not know what more looks like but we know a change is required.

The inmates who make their inner world jumps move into those dark spaces which have haunted them forever and immerse themselves in their overwhelming fear and rage. But they don't act out. Now they tolerate their feelings and watch them and own them and, thereby, heal them. Just by being present to themselves they move through their limitations. Thus, they find freedom and peace inside themselves. They accept their feelings and don't shrink from feeling them. They choose happiness because they acknowledge that they have no good reason to be happy so they must generate their own. Meaning becomes more important than comfort. They can't waste any more time with resentment. So they say "Yes" to life in each moment of each day.

Just as with the inmates, by mid-life those of us who are not incarcerated are challenged to find meaning by delving more deeply into ourselves than we ever have. We risk losing comfort but we acknowledge that we have outgrown the lives we have been living and, truly, we are not comfortable now. For us, too, meaning becomes more important than comfort. And now we find meaning in the moments of our day. We make the mundane sacred by the attention we give it. We practice presence and availability. We, too, say "Yes" to life in each moment. We realize that we have been limited inside our heads and our hearts by a false way of acting and being that promised safety but has delivered compromise.

We can learn from the inmates. Their struggles are evident. Ours are internal but they are the same and require the same courage and commitment.

Mid-Life Hero

Throughout our lives we've made commitments—to study while we were in school, to be faithful, loving and supportive in a primary relationship, and to carry our load at work. Many of us have also made commitments in the interior, personal realm—to heal the parts of ourselves that ached.

The commitment that is asked of us now at mid-life surpasses all those commitments. Now we plunge into the depths inside ourselves we hadn't known existed. Certainly, we've not felt this level of intensity in the compelling pull to get to the bottom of all the craziness we've tolerated and worked around and compromised with. Now there are no more half measures and no more distractions. The pain doesn't seem as frightening as the thought that we may die without having lived authentically and fully and passionately. What was acceptable before—a focus on surviving and prospering materially—is no longer enough.

The power of our wish to have more and to be more emboldens us to venture into those scary places inside because nothing is as scary as the thought of wasting our time on this earth, time that becomes more and more precious with each sunset and each new stiffness and each loss of an acquaintance our age to premature death. Our own death suddenly becomes imaginable in a way that has never seemed quite as real as it does now. The profundity of this whole life experience is overwhelming some days. We can't believe the opportunity we've been given to be alive in this beautiful (or tragic) world and we savor each fleeting second. The importance of loving, whether it's a friend or a pet or a farm or a project, convinces us that commitment from the depth of our being is required and nothing short will suffice.

When we finally commit to living the minutes and the hours of our lives with presence, we enter a realm from which we don't return. We move into a wonderland where we see the life source in ourselves, in others, and in the circumstances we encounter. The correlation between the outside events and inner world conflicts becomes strikingly apparent and we would not consider shrinking from the challenges to live our lives as Heroes.

A Hero lives with integrity and compassion and with a view of the world as her own family. A Hero says, "How can I express the life source that flows through me?" Each moment becomes an opportunity to experience that source as well as to offer it to the world. There is a transpersonal element to living as a Hero. The concerns about "Do I like what just happened" or "Am I getting mine" or "Will I profit from this interaction" fade. With an expanded world view and an appreciation of the finiteness of any one particular life, the Hero's concern is to contribute.

The urgency of "living large" propels us past any fears that have inhibited us in the first part of our lives. The extrovert's fear of her inner world pales when she considers the implications of living without the experience of profoundly and deeply committing to seeing troublesome relationships all the way through, no matter what the cost to herself. The introvert's fear of being known in the world dims when she considers leaving this life with no footprints to chronicle her time here. Whatever our challenge, the need to commit to allowing that life source in us to heal our wounds and fears and hurts is strong, though not irresistible at mid-life.

Always we have a choice. Life is willing to take us where we are and to work with us but we may refuse. If we decide (unconsciously) to curtail the life source by continuing to do what we have always done, if we increase our defenses against the inner tugs and rumblings, then Life gently backs off. We are free to conduct our days as our minds choose, encountering the world as it comes to us and making decisions from our head's knowledge and good judgment. We can rely on past experience to live respectable lives and be law abiding citizens and fit in. But we will be choosing to close off our Hero. While not being derelict or offensive to anyone, we have not grabbed the ring. It's our choice.

The thought of not living to the fullest of my ability and potential scares the beejeebers out of me. I don't want to have regrets after I die. I don't want to hang out with St. Peter and say, "You know, I wish I had tried that," or "I'm so sorry I didn't stand up for my convictions," or "I could have taken more risks."

Mid-life is the time for Heroes. And Heroes are those ordinary folks among us who choose to listen to the life source within and follow it, even when they don't know where they are going. The Hero doesn't concern herself with safety. She needs passion and depth and aliveness. And she realizes that this lifetime and today and this minute are her only opportunities to tell the truth and to be fully alive and to love what is in front of her. So she does it.

MEDITATION

A daily meditation practice opens us to reality within, around, and beyond us. When we sit to meditate, we declare our availability. Meditating from a skeptic's viewpoint means trusting our own experience, not an authority's words.

Throughout the text are italicized meditation instructions. Read them, then close your eyes and experience them.

Getting Started

Your initial meditations may be your mind telling you one thing after another to remember to do. Your response? *Hmmm...* You are just practicing focusing your attention. So any resistance makes for good practice. You watch the lists, the anxiety, the busyness, the feelings, whatever is there. It truly doesn't matter what is there, you just watch. With practice you won't get seduced by the content. Whether the content is pleasing or infuriating or terrifying, it's the process we're concerned with. The act of detaching and focusing attention is all that counts.

> *Imagine that you walk into an empty theater. Choose any seat. Watch what appears on the mind-stage. Memories from an unresolved encounter may be fighting. Daydream fantasies may dance across the stage. Thoughts may lecture you. Whatever happens, just observe. Keep your attention focused on the stage but stay in your seat. Be the Observer. Notice everything but sit and breathe.*

When you look at the contents of your mind on the stage, what do you notice? Watching a stern teacher lecture you is different from being intimidated and taking his words as truth to be obeyed. By watching, we see *what is*. I encourage you not to make a judgment about *what is*, just be aware. So much is going on all the time in our heads and our hearts. When we stop and meditate we turn on the light and notice. Awareness for the sake of awareness is the goal. We are not setting up any struggles, we are not making judgments, we are not molding our characters. We are being and breathing and noticing *what is*.

> *Breathe into any tightness anywhere in your body. Keep your attention focused on that spot and imagine*

your breath going into that place and out from it.
Watch and breathe. Keep your attention focused right
here and allow.

Being present to ourselves may be uncomfortable. There is a reason for the tightness in our bodies. When we give it our attention, we say, I am ready to know you. By meditating we create a space for whatever exists to come forward and present itself. We don't try to understand why our muscles are tight, we just want to be present to the tightness. When we stop, watch, breathe, we invite whatever lives in the tightness to present itself. We are inviting what we are not aware of to become conscious.

If there is pain anywhere in your body, breathe into it
and put your attention there. Just breathe and watch.
Stay present to that place in you, keeping your attention
focused right there as long as you can.

I meditated with a group of chronic pain patients over a period of months. When they focused their attention on their pain and breathed, they reported a shift in their experience of pain. They looked at the energy in their bodies which they had previously labeled as pain, as undesirable, as hated, and just accepted it as *what is* at the moment. They all reported that when they didn't judge their experience or try to change it, it shifted on its own.

Close your eyes and let your breath carry your attention
to any place in your body that needs healing. Your mind
doesn't have to understand where that is. Your breath
will know where to focus your attention. Breathe and
be and notice what is *at that spot.*

Don't try to change anything. In fact, accept what is right there, right now. Stay with this exercise for ten minutes, breathing and being and accepting what is.

We just want to know *what is.* We are impartial Observers, the camera that records, not judges or changes. We are simply practicing being and breathing and noticing *what is.*

As you go through the next hour, maintain this same attitude of noticing without judgment when you look at the outer world and the people you encounter.

What was that like? You may have labeled but not judged. What did you notice about you when you didn't judge others? Some time do this exercise for a day or two and notice the patterns in the labels. Labeling is like taking a picture, it notices but doesn't judge. At the end of a day of noticing and non-judgmentally labeling, tally the number of different labels.

Close your eyes, follow your inhales and your exhales. Breathe and be. Imagine that your attention is focused on a window between your eyebrows and that you are straining to look out. Keep pushing your attention up to and through the window. Label but don't react to what you notice.

When you move through your day as a detached Observer, you will establish a different relationship to your interactions. You will still be the vibrant person you are now but you will add an observing dimension. Thus, you won't be as likely to overreact or to lose your centered stance which you have strengthened through breathing and being. When you do, you know how to move inside and breathe into any space that's disrupted. By knowing the inner world, the outer world becomes clearer.

From your practice as an Observer, you have learned a different relationship to your inner world. Nothing has changed inside you. You notice your inner world activity and keep breathing. You don't have to be dragged around by feelings of which you are unaware. Similarly, you notice your thoughts but you don't have to act on them. *What is* hasn't changed but your experience has. Perhaps the dictatorial controlling voice in your head still barks orders at you, but your response is to notice and keep breathing. Perhaps your anger flashes. Again your response is to notice and keep breathing.

> *Allow your eyes to close and move your awareness to a spot in the center of your body, wherever your breath takes you. Breathe into and out from that place, keeping your attention focused right there. No matter what you see or feel, keep your attention focused and keep breathing. Continue breathing and noticing for twenty minutes. If your thoughts intrude, notice them and release them.*

Write your observations from this exercise in your journal. Notice how the content of your thoughts doesn't determine your reaction to them. No matter what your thoughts tell you, you watch them and breathe. No matter how your feelings impact you, you notice them and breathe. You know in advance what your response is. And when your thoughts tell you that especially in this instance you must do something, you again notice the thought and keep breathing.

This exercise deserves daily practice. What does your mind say about that? Something else to notice.

Realistic Expectations

Meditation allows us to observe *what is*. It doesn't change life. So many times in the last twenty years when I've taught meditation, I've heard comments from students about wanting to avoid pain, to find a way to make life easy by eliminating the challenges, or to get off the emotional roller coaster and always be peaceful.

The danger is that we will adopt another image (Spiritual Seeker, Enlightened Human) and try to mold ourselves to it instead of being present to ourselves. Meditating isn't about the way we talk or dress or what we eat or how we carry ourselves. Meditation doesn't guarantee anything.

Through meditating we learn how to maintain a relationship to our experience that is accepting, grounded, and trusting. Meditating doesn't insure that we won't experience loss and sadness and anger and grief but it does give us a way to move through our feelings.

Meditation offers us a way to approach our inner worlds and a way to learn truths about life. By learning detachment and observation, we can experience anything. We breathe and be and go through the experience. I've found that meditation times can be intensely powerful but that I can endure much more than I thought I could by maintaining my Observer stance and focusing on breathing and being. When you're sitting in a movie theater, it doesn't matter if you're watching a Western, a romantic comedy, a documentary about torture, or a cartoon. You are only the Observer.

Meditation does not create zombies. There is no danger that we will live every minute of our lives with detachment. Exactly the opposite is true. Meditation allows us the berth to experience strong feelings and not lose our centers. We can accept the murderous impulses which scare our rational part and watch them. We can notice that we hold wildly conflicting beliefs and envelop them all. We practice complete self-acceptance.

By teaching us to be present to ourselves, meditation teaches us to be present to others. When we learn to accept without judgment exactly *what is* with another, we deepen our relationships.

> *Allow your eyes to close as they want to. For a few minutes, breathe and be, settling into the stillness. Let your mind be alert and notice your stillness as though it were a blank TV screen. Notice if the screen is clear or fuzzy or chaotic. Breathe into that TV screen until a line is centered and steady. Just watch and breathe and focus on that screen.*

Observing the Mind

Most of us think that our minds are an asset, perhaps our greatest asset. Much of the time they may be. But too often we identify with our minds' creations. We take our thoughts very, very seriously. We are trained to think logically and analytically. If we need to devise a means of moving from one point to another, logical thinking is appropriate. If we want to solve a problem or evaluate alternatives, logic provides the means to proceed.

Life, however, is not a problem to be solved. When it comes to experiencing ourselves in different relationships or with challenges or simply as humans wishing to go through the day with meaning, our minds tend to detract more than enhance. Our challenge in meditation is to watch the mind, not to identify with it or to let it lead us. I have been told numerous times by sincere seekers, "I can't meditate, my mind is too busy." That's exactly why we do meditate. We look at the mind's busyness from a detached perspective.

> Breathe, observing the inhales and the exhales. Imagine that each inhale takes you deeper into your center. From way inside you can look at your mind which seems distant. Watch the thoughts move through your head as though they were clouds moving across the sky. Watch your thoughts, don't think them. Notice them and let them go.

Most of us can look at our thoughts for just a few seconds before we allow them to carry us away. It's funny to think we give our minds permission to diminish the quality of our lives.

Our minds don't tell us that is what they do but we have trained our minds to respond to anxiety with thinking, the only action a mind can take. If our feelings are uncomfortable, our minds take over. Our feelings and thoughts become entwined.

Something in us hates discomfort. We will do almost anything to eradicate it. And we engage our minds in the process. In our young lives we learned to develop intellectual defenses against acting out our impulses. Then we learned to funnel any uncomfortable feeling through our thought waves instead of feeling it. We misused and overused our minds to do a job they were not designed to do. No wonder they torment us with ceaseless activity.

Really, it's touching when I think of the little child-mind in each of us trying to be OK by manufacturing so much intellectual busyness. Whether or not you identify the source of your mind's activity, you know that thinking does not amplify your aliveness.

Think, Don't Be Alive

Our minds' activity reduces our aliveness by reducing our experience of discomfort. Our minds are doing what we asked them to do—to keep us comfortable by using intellectual defenses and distractions. Unfortunately, reducing aliveness by containing one's discomfort in one area results in losing aliveness in every area. It is not given to us to choose when and where we will experience openness to Life. If we are open, we take whatever feeling or experience comes. If we want to close down on that openness, we will reduce our aliveness in every area. It's a package deal.

Life, lived without defenses and distractions, can get pretty intense. Some of my most wrenching experiences have been when I was present to my inner world in meditation. Those times I use my intellect only to provide a structure within which I may move. I "know" how my inner world functions. I "understand" that different levels of my consciousness live simultaneously. With that background my mind provides a time and place to meditate.

Then I leave my mind behind when I move into the inner world in meditation. I give myself over to that world's way of operating and allow myself to be carried. My mind would have me anchored in logic all the time. I release my mind from the job I ask it to do 95% of the day and trust my inner world for these few minutes.

> *As you close your eyes and let your breath pull your attention inside, imagine that your mind drifts up into the clouds. Can you let it go?*

Logic, Trust, and Detachment

The mind and the inner world move in opposite directions. The goal orientation of logical thinking and the experience of trust seem opposite, like being in control versus letting go.

When we let go into meditation, we do so within the framework that our mind provides. Our mind knows that we will breathe and focus our attention inwardly for twenty minutes and then we will return. We do value our conscious, logical process but we know when and where to use that tool. Meditation is not the right arena for the mind. So we look at the mind, not with it. Detachment enables us to look at the mind.

> *Allow your inhales to carry you to that spot in your center, that spot that is most you. Your mind doesn't have to know where this is, your breath knows. Gently release with your exhales and allow yourself to be carried into that center with your inhales. From your center watch the activity in your mind. From your detached perspective notice the different thoughts moving in your head. As each passes, label it and let it go. Watch as it moves out of your head and another moves through. Watch, label, release, breathe.*

When we practice detachment we notice that the thoughts which happen to be moving through our heads lose their urgency to influence us. When we notice them and let them go, they pass. We continue breathing into our centers. We realize that we are not our thoughts. When we look at them and label them, we may not even agree with them. We may be horrified to notice what ugliness exists. When we can look at what we don't like or approve of and keep breathing and keep observing, then we have identified with a deeper spot in ourselves. We know that we are not the thought of the moment any more than we "identify with" the shirt we chose for today. Both the thought and the shirt are something passing and temporary which we don't want to endow with importance.

> *Notice how your thoughts move through you the way your breath moves through you. One thought comes, you notice it, you label it, you release it, and it passes. You observe your breath until you notice another thought, label it, and release it. Do this exercise for ten minutes, noticing thoughts, labeling them, and releasing them. Always come back to the breath to anchor you in that deeper center spot inside you.*

When you watch your thoughts, you notice them but you don't identify with them. You don't take them seriously as though they are real. Does that sound blasphemous to imply that thoughts are not real? Why do we have so many huge universities teaching students to think if their thoughts don't count? Your thoughts are useful in the appropriate context. Now we are speaking about aliveness, consciousness, and being. Thoughts generally do not contribute much to experience in that sphere.

When you watch your thoughts and do not identify with them but just let them pass, you have redefined your relationship with your mind so that you use your mind, not vice versa. Paradoxically, if you want to be in control, meditation is the best way to do so. It dispels illusions that your mind or your will or your accomplishments make a significant difference. It brings you back to your center which is pure being. From there you can observe those thoughts that proclaim that staying in control is important.

> *Let your eyes release their hold on the world as you move inside yourself. Notice that this interior world may be shadowy and undefined. Experience being*

there and breathe. What is it like not knowing what
will happen next? Breathe and wait and stay present
to your experience, watching and releasing.

Accepting that you are not "on top of" your inner world by using
your mind may leave you feeling untethered. What's your reaction?
If you fear your non-rational parts, you may try to eradicate them
or ignore them or devalue them in favor of logic. But in meditation
none of that is relevant. Rational or non-rational, *what is* is the focus
of our attention in meditation. We are present to it all.

Mind Storms

Some days it may feel like you have agreed to take a trip through an ocean storm in a tiny boat. You are tossed about by your thoughts, your to-do list, your worries, and your plans. You may be battered by the force of their demands that you pay attention to them and do it now. So you watch and you breathe and you notice and you release. And they keep coming and keep coming until you think it might be better to just stop meditating for now, do what they want, and come back later.

Please don't!

Your mind is great at finding excuses (and good reasons) not to be present to yourself. That's what it's supposed to do. We thank it for its input and come back to the breath.

> *Close your eyes and breathe for a few minutes. Watch the parade of thoughts that pass through your head. Notice them and their urgency and their words. Do they conjure fear or threaten disaster? How many are there? Label them. Notice that you may not be able to move into your center easily. Just watch all the thoughts march past you and keep breathing.*

Especially when you start meditating, all the meditation may be is watching thoughts, plans, and worries. And realizing that this is not you. Taking the few minutes to detach from this mental chaos in meditation is the finest gift we can give ourselves.

Intellectualizing

Another great distraction the mind suggests is reading about, talking about, or thinking about meditation. At different times you may choose to pursue any of these. They are acceptable ways to spend your time and energy but they are not meditating. Your mind desperately wants to take part in this meditation endeavor and there really isn't much of a place for it once you sit and close your eyes. At that point your mind can only reinforce your commitment to stay in your seat. What's a mind to do?

Perhaps you want to give your mind some time by providing it with reading material but remember to share your time. If you read thirty minutes, spend another fifteen minutes sitting in meditation. Reading is valuable but not sufficient. The experience is what meditation is about and experience by definition is open-ended and unpredictable. Opening to experience, observing what happens, following as you are pulled—this is what meditation is.

> *Allow yourself to relax. Watch the thoughts dance through your head. Notice anything that moves in your head but let it keep moving. As you release any thoughts, worries, plans, allow your exhale to carry off anything you no longer need to hold onto. Notice how you move more deeply into your center. (Or how you don't.) Just notice whatever happens with acceptance and without judgment.*

Is This All There Is?

Many of us felt a gnawing emptiness which we couldn't fill with work, money, love, or prestige. We knew nothing was basically wrong (or so we hoped) but we also sensed strongly that we were missing a vital component of the human experience. Nothing from outside us can fill that hole so it requires turning to our inner worlds.

That is always the last place we look, isn't it, because it's so much easier to blame something/someone outside ourselves. It's more comfortable to look for the coin under the street light than in the shadows where we dropped it. The shadows, however, are ours and a major step in growing up is accepting responsibility for our lives, inner and outer, even when we don't understand what that means or how to do it.

We don't have the answers when we start meditating and by meditating we realize we don't even have the question right. Defining your experience as experience, which meditation teaches us to do, removes us from the realm of judgment or striving. The challenge becomes how to experience *what is* clearly. Nothing else. No comparisons, no what ifs, no how-do-I-do-it-differently. We accept *what is* in this second and don't try to escape it with our minds.

> *Move into your center and breathe for several minutes, becoming aware of what exists right there this second. Focus on that process which exists seemingly independently of you and watch it. At the same time, experience it. Watch and experience. Keep breathing. At this point what do you notice about the ongoing flow of experience in you? Now notice what is this second.*

A Very Personal Journey

I can't tell you what will happen in your meditation and neither can anyone else. Your meditation is yours so you don't need to be concerned with replicating anyone else's experience. You're on a journey of discovery and the world you are exploring exists inside you. It may be the most exciting, powerful, strange, mysterious experience of your life.

I'm serious about those claims. It only depends upon your willingness to let go. A scary concept—letting go—but we only take a baby step at a time. There is no hurry and no prize and no end. There is only today and this minute and your inner world.

> Let your attention move into your center. What's it like in there right now? Breathe into your center and keep your attention focused right there. Watch and breathe and notice what emerges from your center. Life happens there right now. Tune into that life and be present to it. Breathe. Allow yourself to be pulled into this center spot as far as you want. Be present and breathe. Keep your attention focused here, receiving what comes, and observe.

What was that exercise like for you? How does the notion of life going on in your inner world strike you? Could you observe without stopping the flow of life that you saw? In meditation we acknowledge what already exists and, by not judging it or changing it, we allow it to be just as it is. We may not like it and perhaps we're not proud of it. We're just being scientists and noting what reality is. Acknowledging non-physical reality happens beautifully in meditation. We enter a world we didn't choose or consciously create and we accept what we find.

Move into your center. Breathe and observe what is *right now in your center. If there is tightness or pain, breathe into that. Let your breath pull you deeply inside. Watch, listen, and wait. Be present to yourself right now and keep breathing.*

Your inner world already exists. All you need do is become acquainted with it. That's what we do in meditation. Just by knowing it and practicing presence to ourselves, healing ensues. All that's required is openness. Once you show up, the meditative process takes over. Then you just breathe and stay present.

Observing Feelings

Feelings are different from thoughts and observing them requires that we observe the pull they have on us. We feel our feelings at the same time that we observe them—quite a trick. We also acknowledge their pull and observe that, too, without acting. Some of us are thinkers and some are feelers. The latter may have an easier time accessing their feelings. When we meditate, however, feelings are observed, just as the breath and the thoughts are observed. We don't think our thoughts when we meditate but we do feel our feelings, although with some detachment.

Being an Observer of feelings means being firmly grounded in that center spot in you (wherever that may be).

> *Imagine that you are in an airtight, comfortable, safe, and insulated bubble which drops below the surface of the ocean. (If you fear being under water, watch that fear.) The bubble sinks slowly into the ocean, passing below the turbulence on the surface, resting in the calm one hundred yards down. From there you can look at the waves above you but you are not affected by them. Watch and breathe and find the calmness that exists there in your bubble beneath the surface of the water.*

Have you noticed that the center spot in you is always calm? You don't have to manufacture that peace; it exists independently of your mind or your will or your feelings. When you can move past the turbulence, you can move into the already present peace. What a relief! You don't have to create this peace or earn it or work to achieve it. It simply *is* and all you need do is open to it. As we've said before, simple but not easy.

Observe the Distractions

Close your eyes and breathe, watching the inhales and
the exhales. As you focus on the breath notice anything
that arises inside yourself—thoughts, feelings, physical
discomforts, memories, plans, or random fantasies.
Watch them and let them go, bringing your attention
back to your breath. Don't resist, just acknowledge.
Breathe and watch. Always come back to the breath.

Moving into the Scientist/Observer part of you, notice your
experience. How is it to observe this inner world activity? How
do you experience yourself differently when you're identified with
your Observer and not your Thinker or your Feeler or your Doer?
Choosing detachment implies a non-reactiveness which is alert. The
passive Observer watches everything without comment. We know
exactly what is going on, we can name our feeling, we can identify
our conflicts, and we watch. Our eyes are closed but we are alert and
aware of the inner world.

It's easier to notice some feelings in meditation than others. After
meditating for years, I watched rage as it stormed through me. After
twenty minutes/one hour/three hours I then stood up and carried
on with my day. For most of us admitting the existence of ferocious
feelings is threatening and feeling them more so. The beauty of
meditation is that it provides a structure for us to feel what would
be challenging to feel otherwise. I know that when I sit down, I
will breathe and observe. No matter what arises, I will breathe and
observe. No matter how I feel about what arises, I will breathe and
observe. By adhering to this framework, I can acknowledge (and
therefore accept) whatever feelings pass through me.

Breathe into your center for many minutes, feeling
anchored in that peace which exists independently of

your mind. Then let your breath carry you to any spot in your body where there is tightness or pain, physical or emotional. Breathe into that place, putting all your attention right there. Let your breath move deeper into that place. Stay right there and observe. Breathe and watch. Breathe and watch.

This is an exercise you can do whenever you feel a tug and want to be present to yourself to learn what in you wants attention. When we assume the stance of choosing to be present to our inner worlds, we acknowledge everything respectfully. We may label for identification purposes, but we don't judge. We are not embarrassed or proud. We don't react.

Acceptance of *What Is* in our Inner Worlds

Meditation provides us with the attitude of acceptance toward our inner worlds. We don't question whether we like what we see or not or whether we choose to alter *what is*. Meditation increases our awareness of *what is*. Not so we do something about it, simply to notice and experience.

What's the value of noticing? If something ugly exists inside you, wouldn't you rather be oblivious? No. *What is* is. No more denial, no excuses, no rationalizations. We don't have to "come to terms" with *what is*, we just have to acknowledge it and experience it. Why, you may ask, do I have to experience what I don't like, want to be rid of, and will release in the end anyway? Healing requires it. Meditation provides a structure but within this structure we feel what we haven't been able to feel previously. Those old feelings don't disappear just because we don't like them. They stay buried. But in meditation we unearth what has been hidden and feel what we haven't been able to feel before.

> *Imagine that you are descending in an elevator inside yourself. The elevator takes you to an unhealed spot you may not have known was there. Your breath knows where to go. Focus your attention on that spot, breathe, and invite whatever lives there to come. Wait and breathe.*

In meditation what has been buried most recently emerges first. We process the least threatening feelings more easily and the more deeply buried later as we are stronger in our practice. Healing doesn't occur until feelings have been experienced and we can experience them in meditation without anyone ever knowing what is going on with us. No behavior shows on our surface. There may be tornadoes in your chest but your demeanor is still and your eyes remain closed.

Presence Heals

We must experience *what is* that lives in us. Our minds have offered us defenses for all these years so that we could avoid feeling these feelings, but they remain. Experiencing them is the only way we can release them. We can't talk ourselves out of our feelings, we can't rationalize that we are too old to still be feeling this way, and we can't shame our feelings into disappearing. They are ours to experience and until we do, they live.

I meditated with a doctor who told me that he didn't like to work for less than $300/hour. He flew to another city a thousand miles away and back once month for an appointment with a well known spiritual teacher (whose name he dropped frequently). He tried to erase the vulnerability of his youth through his achievements, his money, and his teacher's prestige. Inside him was a quivering six year old who was terrified that he wasn't good enough. The doctor had worked for decades building his defenses against feeling that child's feelings. Then he began meditating. Shortly (predictably) a situation at the clinic at which he worked arose and his position was threatened. His response: intense anger and increased efforts to control. The doctor was unwilling to be present to his fear and so he didn't heal. But meditating always shows us those parts of us which need healing. If you don't want to know your vulnerability, don't meditate. And if you do meditate, stay with it through the storms.

Whatever we fear experiencing will arise when we meditate. Meditating is not a behavior which allows us to remain on the surface and avoid the depths of our beings. Meditating draws to us any situation which supports our healing and, in my experience, that is often turbulent. The doctor feared his vulnerability so that is what he experienced. If we accept what is presented to us, we will heal and that block will disappear. If we react as the doctor did and redouble our defenses, we can continue acting like we meditate, go through the motions, sit with our eyes closed, and impress ourselves. We are not available for healing; we are just using the accoutrements of meditation to enhance our defenses.

Healing in meditation is about partnership. We partner with the previously disowned parts of ourselves by opening to experience the repressed feelings. And we partner with the meditative process when we show up for meditation and accept whatever happens. We create a space during our meditation time for the inner world to show us what needs attention. By meditating we also convey a message to the inner world that we are available to participate in this process.

> *Allow yourself to be available. Notice what it is to relinquish any attempts at control. Your breath will carry you. Watch. Where does your attention go? Breathe into that place and keep your attention right there. Stay focused on that spot for twenty minutes, breathing and accepting whatever feelings arise. No matter what you feel, keep breathing and stay focused right there.*

Vulnerability

Vulnerability may be a dirty word for many of us. Nothing sexual embarrasses, no fears of extreme behavior inhibit. We accept no limitations anywhere except in our relationship to our inner worlds. There we shrink from knowing the depths of our out-of-control feelings. We have acted on the outer world in every way we can. We don't know our inner worlds and our fear of them results in extreme outer world turmoil.

The shadowy inner world terrifies us. Meditation teaches us how to know it, experience its gifts, and learn its language. Humility is required. And then persistence. We persevere through discomfort that we could not tolerate otherwise and we keep breathing. And then a re-organization of how we understand the world emerges from our experience of our depths. Only by being present to ourselves can we truly know what it is to be as fully alive as we can be. Meditation teaches aliveness better than anything I know.

> *As your eyes close, allow yourself to surrender to your inner world where all the rules are different and you don't know the landscape. Move in there as cautiously as you'd like, breathing and keeping your focus on the place in you where you experience feelings. Fiercely keep your attention focused and receive whatever comes. Breathe and feel. Notice each feeling, feel it, and then release it, allowing it to pass. Keep your attention focused on your feeling center and allow the next feeling to arise, feel it while you observe it, and release it as it is ready to move on. Stay with this exercise for twenty minutes.*

Participation

Being the Observer and the Experiencer at the same time is a skill you'll treasure all your life, especially in dicey situations where you don't want to express what you feel at the moment.

> *Can you imagine that you are the Caring Parent holding the Hurting Child, both of whom are parts of you? Feel what it's like to be each part. Your awareness may move between them rapidly. You are not more one than the other. You are both at the same time.*

If you naturally gravitate to one part of you more than another, give the balancing part time in meditation and move between the two. Victims ignore their own Victimizer. Hard Workers ignore their Playful Child. In meditation we encompass everything. All that is exists inside us and is us and we can own that in meditation.

We each have a Shadow—a repository of what we don't like about ourselves and what we have pushed away from our awareness. We each have creative depths which we haven't fully explored. Meditation helps us to integrate our unknown aspects.

> *As your eyes close, surrender to your inner world, allowing it to carry you wherever you need to go. Notice that just as you trust that with each outbreath there will be an inbreath, you trust your inner world to guide your attention. Watch and breathe. Keep your attention focused and receive. Whatever comes is something you need to see. Wait, watch, breathe, and receive.*

Learning detachment and observation allows us to walk through any feelings without identifying with them or being overrun by them.

When feelings are felt they pass naturally. Usually it's our fear of feelings that keeps them around. In meditation we watch that fear, we don't attach to it. When we release the rigidity from our feeling world, we have nothing to resist or act out. We experience a greater trust for our inner worlds and, thus, greater access to our unique creative talents.

The Controller

Have you noticed a tension between your inner world dynamics and your need to be in control? This issue is highlighted in meditation. Too often seekers confuse spirituality (which meditation is about) with religion (which it is not). In scientific terms spirituality refers to the unconscious in all its dimensions, including the personal repressed unconscious, the collective unconscious, and the transpersonal unconscious. It is not necessary to understand any of these constructs. Meditation does not have an intellectual component and it does not profess a creed. Religion refers to a specific set of beliefs and, usually, an institutional structure. Right and wrong are discussed as well as expectations for behavior and thought. Religion promotes an inner Controller who tells you what is acceptable and what is not.

In meditation we don't align with concepts, we lose any agenda for an outcome, and we watch our minds. We enter our meditations not knowing anything. When we are present to our inner worlds and we experience a conflict ("I am angry about the way she spoke to me but I want to be a respectful person so I don't want to act out on my anger but I am steamed and I don't know what to do with myself!"), we stay present and we breathe. We open to our vulnerability and experience the reverberations of our thoughts and feelings in our bodies and our consciousness without making any decisions or taking any action. We learn to tolerate our experience and we just pay attention. We realize that we can't choose what we experience, we can only maintain an attitude of openness to the ongoing flow of experience.

In meditation we practice a relationship to our inner world which is completely trusting and surrendered.

No matter what is *we embrace it and experience it fully.*

We don't solve problems or look for answers or assume that there is a script which guarantees peace. In fact, by staying present to conflicts, feelings, and vulnerability we experience more intensity than our Controller could tolerate. Because we don't have to resolve anything, we can hold everything that exists and let it be. We look at *what is* and by establishing this relationship with our inner worlds we learn that a problem is not a problem if we don't define it as such. It is simply an experience until our Controller tells us it isn't OK and we should eradicate it.

Meditation is about being fully yourself, not about being good or acceptable, just knowing *what is* and experiencing that. Acceptance is the attitude and observing is the behavior. Isn't that perfect for a skeptic? You experience *what is*; you don't criticize it or change it or react to it. You also don't take anyone else's word. You are the authority in your life and you learn how to relate to your own inner world without anyone else's interference.

Regardless of our religious histories, we each have a Controller. For some of us the Controller is huge and for some of us it's tiny. The purpose of the Controller is to keep us safe from vulnerability. Often it does that by telling us to avoid *what is* inside that threatens our appearance of competence. The Controller voice is, like everything else, to be noticed but not to be identified with. We don't give it weight.

> *Close your eyes and follow your inhales and your exhales. Breathe into your center and just observe. If any voice, critical or laudatory, arises, watch is from a distance as though you were across the street. Notice what it says, the tone of voice, and the volume. You may notice your body's reaction to it. Just observe. Breathe and watch.*

The Controller isn't a bad part of us. In fact, we very much need a well-oriented Controller. We just need it in the right place with the right job assignment. I put my Controller in charge of financial records, housecleaning, and car maintenance. When she speaks to me about other matters (I can tell it's my Controller because my shoulders tighten), I thank her and re-direct her attention. The Controller is not for Adults to listen to about their worth as humans. It's a technician with skills appropriate to confined tasks.

In meditation the Controller has a place by reinforcing the commitment to daily meditation (if that is your Adult's decision) and by providing a place for it. You don't need to hear your Controller's comments about meditative behavior. Bragging about how many minutes/hours you meditated or where or with whom pulls you away from your center and your being and distorts the meditation process to serve as an ego boost. Meditation is not about ego and not about doing anything right and not about being good. We don't meditate because we hope some Higher Power will smile on us. We meditate to be present to ourselves. Not for honors, not for rewards, not to impress, simply to be.

> Allow your eyes to close. Breathe, following your inhales and your exhales. If your mind tells you to do something, notice that thought, label it, and release it. Breathe. There is nothing to do and no place to go right now. No thoughts are needed, but all are noticed and released. Stay with your breath, noticing and releasing all thoughts and feelings. Breathe and be.

How unproductive is that? Spending time breathing and being. Infants do that. Are we imitating infants? No. There are pre- and trans- qualities to meditation. In our very early life we had yet to develop our individuality. Growing up, we did, and now as adults we realize that there is more to us than our minds and our feelings and our personalities and definitely more than our achievements and how the world sees us. We may have so many layers of defense built up inside that we have lost connection with that spark from our essence, that being-ness that lives in our core.

> *As you close your eyes and breathe, move your identification deeper and deeper within, past your Thinker, your Do-er, your personality. Let the breath carry you into that place where you simply be. Breathe and be. Let yourself move even more deeply into that spot. You may notice that you pass through a fine scrim. On the other side, you share in a sea of beingness with every other being. Be there and breathe. You have released your sense of your own separate individuality. Now you may not identify with an "I" as much as with the ongoing flow of being. Just be in this ocean of being-ness.*

Losing our boundaries is definitely not something the Controller encourages. But with experience meditating you will find yourself more aware of "being" and less concerned with "I." Your sense of participation in Life becomes less one of a separate ego and more one of participating in the whole. This "self-image" based on belonging greatly reduces a sense of stress which may have developed from the Controller's fear-based injunctions.

> *As your eyes close and you breathe, let yourself gently drift away from the world as you know it. Allow yourself to float into a space that's foggy, as though you're inside a cloud and can't define the outline of yourself or anything else. You breathe in this fog and your outbreath becomes the fog. Fog around you and fog within you. The fog you breathe in moves through your body. The breath you breathe out becomes the fog.*

Can you allow yourself to melt into the fog, letting the
cells of your body gently dissipate? Keep breathing and
see this dissipating process happen as long as you can.
If you can't see it, watch whatever comes up.

I'm not suggesting that this experience is necessary or valuable but
it is one that many of us have had in meditation. You may have it,
too, or you may not. It doesn't matter. Meditation teaches us about
reality and this lesson concerns fluidity and oneness. You'll open to
it when you're ready. Don't try to replicate it or resist it. Just know
that it may happen. All that's really important is for you to stay with
your own process.

Observing the Controller

I discuss this issue here because it is a Controller issue. Meditation will confront all your Controller issues. One Sunday I walked with a friend through a state reserve. It was a lovely day with many strollers. As we talked we passed a couple sitting quietly. The man jumped up and yelled at us, "Can't you see we're meditating?" He and the woman glared at us.

They had been given the perfect opportunity (perfect by our disruptive presence) to look at their Controllers but instead they identified with the Controllers' ire and unreasonable need to control what it could not. Life can't be tailored according to Controller specifications for long. And when you accept that it can't, and that Life knows better than you what is right for you, you've moved to a level of surrender in your partnership with Life.

> *Breathe and be still. Focus all your attention inside*
> *in your center. Breathe into that spot and just listen.*
> *Wait receptively.*

In meditation we ask the Controller to wait at the door. She gets us into our seats and then leaves. Should her voice come up in our meditations, we notice it and gently show her the door. The meditative experience is one which we jump in and then let go. We don't know what will happen, we don't even try to influence it. We don't recite words to structure our experience. We show up, we breathe, and we stay present.

Trusting Life

It's a miracle, isn't it, that Life knows exactly how to respond to us when we choose to sit. Meditation is so intensely personal that much of the experience cannot be understandably communicated. Often we won't even know for ourselves what happened until later. For a skeptic, this may sound pretty undefined. It is, but so is getting married or joining Toastmasters or going to college or having a child. We sign up for an experience and then agree to let it happen.

> *Let your eyes close when you are ready. Move your attention inside, taking as long as you need to move out of your thoughts, away from your feelings, and into that center space. Breathe and be and notice what it is to be yourself right now, this second. Breathe into your center and stay present to yourself. Whatever you notice is OK. Whatever you feel is fine. What is it like to be you right now? Watch and release. Breathe, watch, release.*

Just watching what goes on inside us is revelatory.

> *Right now I'm going to give my inner world my full attention. I want to be present to that being that I am and shine the light of my awareness on my momentary experience. I know that being present to myself this second is the most life-enhancing choice I can make.*

Certainly, the Controller would have a comment for that one! And your challenge is to look at that comment and know that your Controller is doing the best job she can and that she loves you very much. She's just coming from fear with a narrow view of the world and of you in it. When we think about consciousness/being we move out of the Controller's arena. She may yell very loudly because, after all, she wants to be In Control. That's what she does. So we watch her and appreciate her and realize her limits.

The Hero

The opposite of the Controller is the Hero. We each have a Hero wanting to emerge. The Hero moves into the world (inner and outer) and experiences whatever comes. He has a purpose greater than himself. He is not trying to be safe but to be all he can be, to trust that which invites him to be larger than he has ever been. The Hero acknowledges the pull which demands that he surrender his small identity. By letting go, he opens to being carried.

> *Imagine that you walk up to a hot air balloon which is ready to float away, except that the basket is tethered at each of its four corners. If you are willing, climb into the basket. Release the first tether when you are ready. Follow your breath and notice* what is *in your center. Take your time and release as many of the other tethers as you are comfortable releasing. Can you let yourself float? Can you let the hot air balloon carry you? Breathe into your center and stay focused there while you watch this scene.*

The Hero says "Yes" to life. If he is afraid, he takes his fear with him in his explorations. Inner world explorations are often more challenging than outer world travels. Your Hero faces every challenge, knowing that his purpose is to partner with Life, not to shrink from his challenges. The Hero commits to living with integrity, awareness, and openness. When he enters meditation, it is with an attitude of welcoming whatever comes, no matter how it feels or what the Controller says. Commitment is the hallmark of the Hero.

> *Let your breath take you into your center. Each inbreath carries you further into this place. Invite your Hero to guide you. Walk, holding your Hero's hand.*

What comes into your body from his hand? Let your breath nurture your courage.

The Hero's journey is completely personal in meditation and noble in its intent. He's not ambitious. He is surrendered to a pull that he senses strongly but may not understand. He relies upon surrender and trust. He opens to Life to teach him. Meditation is the ideal format for experiencing your Hero and allowing him to lead your way. Any blocks to your Hero (fear, pettiness) are acknowledged, observed, and released.

Meditation allows you to open to everything inside yourself. The Hero is one part just as the Controller is. Each part contributes to the meditative experience in its own way.

The Outer World as a Mirror

Now that you have practiced identifying with the fluid "being core" in your center, you've probably noticed that your inner world is very much an active scenario, with all sorts of feelings, thoughts, Controller injunctions, and Hero tugs floating around. As a skeptic, you may find that fascinating. I do. I love watching all this action that isn't scripted or pre-determined. I am the only Observer who is privileged to enter this world. No one can tell me what is what or what I "should" do or even what the rules are, for I discover my own inner world rules as I meditate.

So, only you can notice the relationships which already exist inside you since you are the only scientist in your laboratory. Is there a struggle between your Controller who tells you not to need or want or be vulnerable and another part of you who very much wants and does feel fragile sometimes?

In the inner world we know that everything we see and experience is part of us. We learn a different relationship to the parts of us. We learn to observe and acknowledge and accept. We don't take any part too seriously and we don't react. We learn to move into our ever peaceful centers and breathe and allow. Meditation helps us to understand that reality flows and changes. It also teaches us to let go.

What is, whether that be anxiety or anger or depression, may not change but our relationship to it is one of tolerance. We don't fight our experience or judge it. We learn to experience and let go. Whatever happens then is OK.

Observing the Outer World

Just as you learn to notice your inner world in meditation by adopting the stance of non-reactive Observer, you use that same detachment to watch *what is* in your outer world. You are an Observer in each.

> *Let your breath carry you into your center. Be there and breathe. Allow your breath to carry you deeper into that place of peace which exists independently of your mind. Breathe and allow that peace to move through your body. Maintaining your anchor in that peace, gently allow your eyes to open. Observe the outer world as you breathe into that peaceful center and out from it.*

Do you notice a difference in your seeing when you are anchored in that inner place of peace? The scrim we usually see through is what we focus on in meditation. As we meditate distortions in our scrim are reduced, like cleaning our glasses, so that the world may then appear to be different even though nothing outside of us has changed.

You've noticed the dynamics characteristic of your inner world— Controller injunctions, intense feelings, recurrent thoughts. When you look at the outer world, do you notice those same dynamics? What is similar about your inner world and your outer world? If you were to take the outer world as a manifestation of your inner world and walk through your day as though you were walking through your inner world in meditation, I wonder what you might notice.

> *Follow your inbreath into your center and out through your center as it pulls you into a neighborhood. Notice the buildings and the landscape. How does it feel being in this world? Watch what happens, whom you meet,*

*and how you're treated. Maintain your detachment
and observe.*

Notice your experience in the outer world this week. At the end of each day describe in your journal three occurrences that stand out. Which psychodynamics were involved? Again, use your labels.

Life

Perhaps you question why I include a discussion of psychodynamics and the outer world in a book about meditation. In meditation you learn to know yourself without judgment. By implication you learn about the world. You have observed your inner world without controlling and you noticed how Life has provided its own direction. You have noticed your Hero's willingness to trust Life and to surrender.

Now when you look at the outer world you may notice your reflection in the difficult people you encounter. You may see that the ocean of being-ness has its very real, mundane implications. Maybe you've noticed that when you're tense, nothing moves as easily for you. When you trust, doors open and parking spaces appear. (Do your own experiments to verify this.) When you are frustrated by not effecting what you want in the outer world, look inside for what you are not seeing there.

We've already spoken about consciousness (is-ness) as an ocean in which we all float. Our little individual consciousness merges with everyone else's. When we are not clear in ourselves and allow distorted thoughts or feelings to dominate to an unhealthy degree, it affects our consciousness which then impacts the ocean. The Hero conceives of his job as keeping his three square feet of ocean clear and he does that by meditating to allow healing of outdated beliefs and unhealed wounds. His responsibility to the whole demands that he do his own inner work. Sitting in meditation is not navel gazing but is acknowledging the oneness of existence and our own individual responsibility to the whole to clean up our own consciousness.

> *Breathe into your center and be. Let the inbreath*
> *flow through your center. Let your outbreath release*
> *whatever you no longer need to hold onto. Your breath*

will do the work. As you breathe and you notice your breath moving through you and out, notice how your field of influence grows. With each breath your limits expand. Watch that happen for several minutes. You breathe in and your outbreath fills the room. Keep breathing and notice that your outbreath fills the whole house and then the block and the neighborhood and your state. Eventually, your breath covers the nation and the globe. Keep breathing and notice.

Meditation shows us *what is* inside us and our influence (unconsciously) on *what is* around us. By working with consciousness we are operating on a very fine level. When we see the correlation between the inner world and the outer world, we realize that if we want to change the outer, all we need to do is work with our own consciousness.

A distortion in our own consciousness may be manifesting as a form in the outer world which we don't like to see. The meditator's first response when she sees something that offends is,

How is this showing me myself?

We don't criticize another or yell or engage in a struggle with the outer world. We look inside and meditate. *Whatever is* is perfect. We may not understand how, but all is consciousness and meditation is the fastest way to work with consciousness.

Breathe into your center and be. Focus your attention on your center and be present to whatever is there right now. Breathe and be. Stay present to yourself, acknowledging everything—your thoughts, feelings, memories, plans. Release and keep breathing. Continue doing this exercise for twenty minutes.

When the outer world seems out of balance, we do well to look for the imbalance inside. Our breath will correct the imbalance if we stay focused. Not our minds, not our actions, not our wills. Simply breathing with focused attention will allow any distortions to arise. Just by seeing them and holding them in awareness while we meditate, they are healed.

Life is a precise Healer. Participation with Life in this process requires humility which shows in acceptance and surrender. We accept *what is* and we surrender our wills so that we don't know what is coming next. We don't try to force anything. As we've learned in meditation, we sit with openness and commitment and we wait. As we walk through Life, we don't know what comes next but we accept everything. We trust that Life will bring us the lessons we need in order to heal and grow.

> *Breathe into your center, focusing on your inhales and your exhales until your thoughts become quiet. Watch whatever then arises with respect and detachment. What do you notice? Let the breath carry you deeper within. Again, watch. And move deeper. Focus on the breath until a thought or feeling arises and then watch until it passes.*

Notice what stands out for you in your inner world forays and your outer world encounters over the next week. Be a Scientist/Observer with no stake in the outcome.

Meditation starts as a twenty minute exercise but it evolves into a lifestyle. Meditation teaches us a way of thinking and experiencing life and ourselves. It provides an orientation which lends meaning to our experience. Without trying, we see connections, we know in ways other than intellectual, and we allow our wounds to heal. Meditation leads us to partnership with Life.

Presence and Passion

Meditation teaches us to be present to ourselves and to Life. Presence is awareness of *what is* at the moment and total acceptance of that while we experience it. It is a full-bodied, arms-thrown-wide-open YES! The YES is our response to life. It is our acceptance of anything that exists and our choice to be fully affirming of our experience, no matter how we feel about it or what we think about it. It is our complete acceptance of the moment, the stance that says no matter *what is* I accept it and I affirm it and I embrace it. I choose to partner with Life and not fight or whine or otherwise avoid living fully whatever today brings, knowing that reality is both internal and external.

This open-hearted response, taking our fear with us, underscores our commitment to being fully alive. Meditation offers us practice at living without constraints or inhibitions. What greater gift could you want? Having every fiber of your being awake and responsive at each moment is the most you can choose.

Because we learn to observe and to tolerate our experience, we can relinquish our defenses which close down our experience of life. We developed defenses against our aliveness when life was too much for us and we wanted to limit our experience. Now that meditation has taught us how to observe and breathe and accept and release, we no longer need to close down. Nothing threatens our aliveness. We can handle whatever comes to us with the skills that meditation teaches.

> *Allow your eyes to close and for a few minutes breathe, watching the inhales and the exhales. As you move into your center, see yourself walking down a path. Notice your surroundings and keep walking. Notice other living beings in your imagery, human and non-human. Several figures approach you as you continue*

walking. Watch. What do you notice about the
approaching figures and about your reaction?

Recording your experiences after meditating may help anchor the meditative reality into which you've dropped. What have you learned about reality and your place in the world? How is the world defined and limited by your mind? What have you learned about non-physical reality?

> *Breathe into any part of your body that is tense or*
> *hurting. Focus on that spot for several minutes,*
> *watching the inhales and the exhales, seeing the breath*
> *going directly into that spot and out from it. Keep*
> *all your attention right there. Watch your breath go*
> *through that spot, through your center, down your*
> *legs, and into the center of the earth. Watch as your*
> *outbreath returns and moves up your legs and back*
> *through your center and into the original spot. Notice*
> *what is different.*

The creativity of your inner world is unlimited. When you learn to trust it, to surrender to its pull, and then to receive its direction, you have a reliable compass for navigating through the day's choices. You also "see" the reality behind the form just as you learned to do by observing *what is* behind the thoughts and feelings.

> *Close your eyes and breathe for several minutes,*
> *allowing your attention to move inside. Feel yourself*
> *pulled down a path. After several minutes you notice*
> *an obstacle blocking your path. Walk up to it. What*
> *is it? Watch and notice how you move beyond the*
> *obstacle.*

Meditative imagery shows you the creativity of your inner world. Visual imagery may or may not appear to you. All that is important is that you know the language of your own inner world. Practice meditating will teach you that. There is no one better to spend time with than yourself and no one who can be more present to you.

> *Again as you move into your center, notice what it is to be you this minute. Breathe and be. Imagine your source being lifted straight up so that you are looking down at yourself from a distance of several yards. And then a mile. What do you notice about the being who is sitting in meditation? Can you see her perfect core?*

Could you look at that figure (who is you) with detachment and appreciation? Did your Controller's voice intrude? Is it possible to lose all sense of ownership when you acknowledge yourself as a being in the world? Is your sense of yourself changing?

> *Moving your attention inside, allow your Observer to assume prominence. Invite your Observer to recline on a beautiful deep red magic carpet. Watch as the carpet floats up to the clouds and over the last week. Is there any troublesome interaction your Observer views from this vantage point which looks different from how it appeared when you first lived through it?*

When you think about moving through your days as an Observer, you lose some of the urgency and relentless drive that we achievers have mastered. Simply being in the Observer position implies that Life is OK and doesn't require our direction and control. Moving through Life without a goal and without even attempting control seems somehow irresponsible. I suggest that that is the most responsible stance we can assume. We defer to a reality greater than our minds can comprehend, we acknowledge our part in it, and then we wait for guidance from within.

I offer you this thought assuming that you have a Controller to release: shifting our identification away from the Controller and the mind is not a refutation of the value of this part of us. It is simply taking the next step. After we have excelled in our intellectual and organizational and management skills and the duties of daily life are accounted for, then we move into the next phase by letting go. We can trust our inner worlds since we have spent so much time meditating and listening.

> *Close your eyes and breathe into your heart. Stay there in your heart for several minutes. Does the breath move into your heart easily? Can you see it circulating there? Is it blocked anywhere? Keep breathing into your heart and keep your attention focused right there. Stay with this exercise as long as you can.*

We've learned how to handle anything that arises—we simply observe, breathe, and keep our attention focused. No matter what pain, what excitement, what intensity, the pattern is the same— observe, breathe, focus. We approach our experience in this way. The point is not to live in a detached fashion or to become a zombie or to deny our needs.

We meditate so that we live more fully than we ever have and more fully than we could if we didn't meditate. Meditation is about passion and complete immersion in life and the willingness to lose our little individual ego (temporarily) so that we may experience more than we could otherwise. We let go to receive. We don't "order" our experience, we just accept it and live fully. Saying *Thank you* facilitates this process.

Paying Attention

A practice I find useful more than once a day is to stop and ask myself, What am I paying attention to now? If I'm thinking, I wonder what is behind the thought. If I'm frustrated, I ask what I need to see that I don't. If my body is tense, I look for a hidden belief.

Asking myself, What am I paying attention to, is not inviting the mind to perform its antics. It does the opposite. It grounds me in what is real by helping me to see through the bluster of my thoughts to the underlying reality.

What are you paying attention to now?

> *Moving inside you on the breath, watch and listen and wait. Notice* what is *this second in your center? And this second? And this second? Be present and notice and breathe, experiencing it all.*

SPIRITUALITY

When we experience ourselves moving in a larger flow, noticing the reflections and the reverberations inside and around us, we play with the Universe. We notice coincidences, directions, and guideposts. We see responses to our thoughts and choices. We know we belong. And always we pay attention to the reality greater than ourselves.

Breathe and Be

"Breathe and be and stay focused on this second." I find myself saying those words repeatedly in the daily guided meditation groups. Folks with no or much experience meditating convene to sit for forty-five minutes. I speak a few words as they come to mind for the purpose of anchoring our attention.

Paying attention to *what is* each second challenges our jumpy minds. Learning to simply *be* in the Observer while practicing detachment invites an alert passivity. We sit, we breathe, we notice our breath, our thoughts, our feelings, and we sit and we breathe and do it again. We stay in our seat and just notice what unfolds. We may like what we're shown or not. It doesn't matter; we just watch

We notice our thoughts and our feelings but we maintain our detachment. We don't start thinking and we don't identify with our feelings. We breathe and watch and stay in our Observer. Learning detachment allows us to identify with the Observer, a part of ourselves deeper than our thoughts and feelings.

Newcomers to meditation often struggle with their inner world chaos. "I can't meditate; my mind is too busy." "That's exactly why we meditate," I respond. Meditation isn't quieting the mind. It's having a different relationship to it—one in which we look at our thoughts instead of identifying with them. The same with feelings—we notice them while we experience them. Our Observer maintains its detachment and watches the whole show from a bit of a distance.

Sometimes I use the image of the Observer looking through a window. On the Observer side of the window, the breath comes and goes naturally as though the breath is breathing us. We be, we notice, and we allow. On the other side of the window, thoughts and feelings move. Staying on the Observer side of the window, we look at them without being caught up in thinking or feeling. We notice the anger or the frustration or the joy or the excitement or the worries or the plans or the memories and we allow them to pass. We don't attach to anything.

When we identify with the Observer part of us, we notice our Critic (on the other side of the window) through the angry self condemnations. We notice our Controller with its shoulds. And always we notice our Child. We notice everything and we allow. We practice allowing in meditation by staying in the Observer, breathing, being, noticing, and releasing.

"I want to do something. I don't like these feelings!" Another thought to notice. Only by noticing and allowing do we experience healing. We allow without resistance and, thereby, we cooperate with Life. Our minds are not required in the healing process; surrender and trust are. When we practice surrender and trust we operate in partnership with Life. Life always wants to bring us to healing. We allow healing in meditation.

Lost and Found

Times of challenge are followed by times of overcoming. It seems that this is the rhythm of life. Always we learn about letting go. We don't need to add on, to learn more, to increase—we need to release what interferes with our being authentically ourselves.

Unconsciously, we have covered over our natural clarity with what we hoped would make life easier—our wit, our intellectualism, our attractiveness, our compliance, or, perhaps, our ability to intimidate. We didn't want our vulnerabilities to be noticed; we thought we weren't good enough. We wanted to be safe and we thought that increased defenses provided the answer—keep folks away from those tender areas and we'll never hurt or fear.

But the result is that we are not comfortable with ourselves in a new way. Before we feared the intensity of our natural feelings; now we may not know what we feel. So, in addition to others not knowing us, we don't even know ourselves! We never integrate our vulnerabilities and, therefore, we don't experience their great gifts and potential. We choose to live a two dimensional life instead of exploring our own depths.

Why do we think we would be better if we are less ourselves?

We have added so much onto ourselves in the course of living every day that sometimes it's challenging to get back to the essence of who we are. We have covered shame with bravado. We have hidden fear with sarcasm. We have ornamented our surroundings so that distractions endlessly pull our attention.

But at our very center lives the light which has always been there and always will be. That's what we really want—to live from our center honestly and without pretense. We already have Source at our center.

We don't need to earn Source or deserve Source or find Source or satisfy Source. We are expressions of Source. The problem is we are so much more.

Realizing our Source essence may be overwhelming. To think that we have power of that dimension inside us this second can be breathtaking. Do we really want that kind of power? If we truly acknowledge that right now this minute we are Source, we can't let ourselves off the hook. It's not a pressure to behave in a certain way. Realizing our essence is accepting our unlimitedness.

Why would we refuse that?

Because it scares the bejeebers out of us! Right now this minute saying "Yes, I am Source" and "Yes, I am unlimited" implies that we have all we need this minute. There isn't a struggle and there isn't a problem. This is it and I am it and there's nothing to wait for. No one is coming to save us. There is nothing outside ourselves to seek. All the gifts and the riches and the power reside within us this second. When we lose our self-constructed facades, we find ourselves.

A Deeper Level of Forgiveness

This is the year. I'm finally going to do it this year. I'm not wasting any more time. I'm not indulging any more delays. This is the year I am exploring forgiveness at a depth I've here-to-fore not mastered.

I can allow others to be confused or insensitive or preoccupied. I've learned to not take slights personally. I can overlook the intermittent disappointment.

But there is a level of forgiveness I've yet to practice. And that has to do with releasing my Child's hold on HUGE hurt feelings. In my Adult I can forgive anything because when I'm in my Adult, nothing gets too far in. I can handle it intellectually or verbally or interpersonally. But the Child's feelings are overwhelming and pre-verbal, necessarily unutterable. They have to do with my very existence, with the validity of the core of my being. In my Child I can be wiped out, just demolished. I imagine that the parts of me vaporize and float away and that I no longer exist.

How can I forgive when my very existence is at stake?

Because my existence is not at stake. It feels like it is to my Child, but what I know as an adult that I could not know as a child is that the light at my core is not diminished, no matter what anyone does or says. Words hurt my feelings or my sense of belonging in the world. But no words destroy the integrity of my essence.

At my core I am one with Source. No one created that and no one can destroy that. Verbal or physical insults don't reach that deeply. And no matter what anyone thinks of me and no matter who hates me and no matter how badly I'm treated, I am one with Source.

And from that place I can forgive anything. What detracts at that core level? Nothing human or passing. Certainly, I don't need to be concerned with someone else's judgments when I identify with my Source consciousness. And I don't judge from that consciousness. Not anyone else and not myself.

I can forgive anything and everything. As long as I'm in my Source consciousness. All I have to do is to choose that. It's always there.

Grace

Grace is a beautiful word, but what does it mean in practical terms for us today? It sounds like melted chocolate that covers an entire situation and turns it sweet. Or a gentle fog that erases the rough edges. I am open to receiving a blessing like that. Nothing similar to that has ever happened to me, though. The situation doesn't transform and the world doesn't soften.

What has happened, and I only see this in retrospect, is that situations in which I have lost—ie, situations I couldn't make turn out "right," gave me a new way of seeing. Initially, I fought and struggled both with others and in my mind. I didn't want to be a loser and I needed "them" to validate me. I wanted them to see how right I was. When I couldn't wrest that understanding and acknowledgement from the other, I felt frustrated. I also felt diminished in worth. I allowed the other person to define my value. And I hated him/her for not assessing me as I wanted!

Often I spent months regurgitating the sad events, much longer, I am sure, than any other person thought about me. If I could just think long enough and hard enough, I could make the past turn out right! It never worked.

And then I considered grace. My definition of grace is when I am propelled from one level of consciousness to another, a higher one. I am not a winner at one level. But I am committedly on my own side; my belief in myself never wavers. The truth is I don't need anyone's understanding or acknowledgement. And if I don't receive acceptance, I move on. It's OK to let go. Even in relationships that are supposedly foundational—family, love, authority relationships. If I try to "straighten them out" (read: be seen) and I can't, I take it as a sign that I'm not supposed to be there.

Life is for learning and growth and change. Finishing third grade led to celebration. Why doesn't finishing chapters of my life result in celebration? Others may not be ready to move on but my timing originates deep within me. Something in my core seems to know me even more deeply than my mind does. And in committing to listen to that guidance, I am often led in an unpredictable direction.

It has taken me decades to find that whisper in my essence but that is the part of me I can trust. I never run into a wall there. Sometimes I am forced to stop and look at something I have ignored. But with that attention, change and growth always open something new.

Grace teaches me to stay on my own side, never doubting but always paying attention. Grace leads me to let go and trust my essence more than my mind. And grace always carries me to another level. Grace confirms me, often not gently, but always respectfully. I find understanding and acknowledgment from the grace that guides me.

Erecting the Barrier

Will you please join me for a few minutes in the presumption that although we say we want a relationship with Source, in fact, that is not true. That basically we don't want to know or be known by Source, we don't want to lose our boundaries and our separateness and our uniqueness, we don't want to disappear into the larger whole as one drop disappears into the ocean.

Building our Controller takes time and work and comes out of disappointment or hurt and is designed to insure safety. In the first part of our lives, we all prefer safety. Then we reach our 50's and suddenly safety seems like a coffin and we are not ready for that quite yet. And the balance shifts in the safety vs. unpredictable-aliveness dichotomy. I have heard many people say that they started their spiritual practice originally out of great pain, with hopes of ending their suffering and finding a path that kept them safe from hurt. They expected Source to be an analgesic. They subscribed to the butterflies and sunshine theory of spirituality: if I am good, Life will be easy.

This is a stance most of us outgrow. When we see that we can't manipulate Source into giving us what we want, we may assume an attitude of never-mind-I-will-take-care-of-myself. And by the way, screw you, Source, for not being what I want. This is a good platform for building a Controller. We can erect an image of ourselves that is hard to see through, that erases vulnerability, and that is generally admired. How long we dally in this stage is related to the success of and the rewards we receive for doing our Controller number. It's possible to live an entire lifetime here.

For those of us fortunate enough not to be too successful, we move on to, "OK, so I really can't do it on my own. I need help." This is said with a sigh of resignation which is not surrender. Our Controllers haven't really released the strings. We do "spiritual" acts but our hearts are not present. We putter along without experiencing the depth and intensity of our feelings. We're still relating to ourselves in a superficial way and hoping that that will suffice. It is only when we have lost all hope, when we know we can't survive on our own, when we can't even find the path, much less make our way down it, when we lose hope in everything we have known, when we are shattered beyond apparent repair, that is when we can approach Source.

What does Source want with our Controllers and our success and our self-congratulations? Those are just barriers which keep us from knowing Source. When we truly want a relationship with Source, when we are finally clear that we can't live our lives meaningfully and satisfactorily on our own, when we know that there is more we must have but don't know what it is or how to get it, when we can't play the game anymore and have released our Controller's claims to worthiness and safety, only then are we ready to stand naked and undefended, and say, "I am here, ." And then we wait.

Source isn't far away but is in the deepest cells of our being. Source is deeper in us than our bone marrow and more essential to our being who we are. So after we have spent most of a lifetime getting away from our weakness and vulnerability and sadness, we are thrust right back. Into it.

And that is where Source waits for us.

It's funny, isn't it, that what we can do for ourselves isn't of much interest to Source. It is not a teacher with rewards for work but a lover who says, "Give me your heart." Personally, I would rather do something any day than just be and trust and feel all that ensuing anxiety. Having Source say, "I am here, let me love you," makes me nuts. I want to say, "Yes, I am here, or at least I will be this afternoon after I've made some phone calls. And as for loving me, well, I'm still in process, Source, and I'm working on this anger thing and I've almost got it, so let's just wait a week and then I will really be ready for your love. Don't give me too much now. I don't want to lose my momentum. Not too much joy or prosperity or, heaven forbid, love from another human. I'm not quite ready yet, but I promise you, I'm working on it."

Source hears, "I'm not available." And accepts that. So, we are the ones (entirely) who decide how full a relationship with Source we open to. It is always there. Granted, the terms are harsh and it seems like through the first part of our lives, they get harsher and more demanding. Maybe Source tolerated us doing our Controller number out in the world in our 20's and 30's but by our 40's, Source says, "Come on now. What about those parts of you that you left behind? You remember that sadness from your childhood that you never did heal? What about feeling that now?"

We can't separate ourselves from any parts of ourselves— uncomfortable feelings, perceived weaknesses, fears, vulnerabilities— without separating ourselves from Source. Source is not on the altar in a cathedral with a sparkling chandelier. Source is in the darkest, most hateful spot in our hearts, waiting, hibernating, but not dying or disappearing. Source will be patient for just so long and then It demands that we look where we have avoided looking, that we acknowledge what we have denied and tried to kill inside ourselves. Source is not in the shiny facade of the mansion; It is in the closet behind the door, under the clutter, in the dusty corner of the basement.

And that's where we have to be, also, if we want to be present to Source in us. It waits for us and calls to us softly at first and then increasingly loudly, through our bodies' aches and our drinking and our tears and our broken relationships. That's where we find Source and where It waits and will always wait. Only when we go back to our messes, can we find our experience of Source.

Source is to be experienced, not talked about. Even though "knowing" is an intellectual word, knowing Source is an experience, not an intellect-driven endeavor. When we stay in our heads we avoid experiencing Source and we avoid experiencing the deepest parts of ourselves. It is only when we dare to immerse ourselves in our passion and let it carry us that we are open to experiencing Source. As long as we feel in control, we don't need Source. Allowing ourselves to need, to know that we are not whole in and of ourselves, is the first step. Realizing that we cannot do what we need to in order to make our lives complete is unsettling. The further realization that what is required is unknown and out of our grasps prove to be terrifying.

By the time we have been beaten down and discouraged and hopeless, we realize that we cannot make our life turn out "right" by our own efforts. Then surrender doesn't seem impossible. In fact, it is the only door open. How much more can we hope and try and how long will we bloody our heads against the wall that we are now seeing we have erected? How many heart attacks are enough before we change? How many lost loves before we say, "What I need I can't get from anyone else?" What does it take before we are ready to concede that while this ego ride has its moments, it is not a long-term satisfying way to live. Only a life based on a strong personal relationship with Source offers that and that isn't something that can be received from outside. It can't be bought or earned or given in a church. No matter who your teacher is, it doesn't come from outside. It's strictly an inside job and Source waits for us inside, not where you want It to be and not in the way you prefer.

Source always chooses what is our least together area, our most unfocused point, and then demands that we live out of that. None of our worldly successes are any help and, in fact, the defenses we have created hinder us in knowing Source in personal terms. That is what is required–a commitment to a complete, full, total relationship with Source. No holds barred, no escape routes open. Everything is on the line and there is no safety net.

And from that point we say, "I am here and I'm paying attention."

We simply stand and we be and we breathe and we wait. And that's it. We don't know what to expect and we no longer think of trying to control or limit *what is*.

"I am here and I am available."

Divine Discontent

Growing up Catholic, I was taught that we make some decisions that are immutable—marriage, for instance. Once you are married there is no divorce and no remarriage in the Church (in the 60s). Once a man or woman religious takes vows of obedience, s/he relinquishes self-determination. Assumed was an attitude that what exists at one moment in time will persist.

However, humans grow and learn and expand without conscious choice. We experience life, we adjust, we refine our attitudes, we experience more, we make mid-course corrections, we try something new, we reconsider our options, noticing some we hadn't previously acknowledged, and we keep going. Challenges bombard us. We re-evaluate our choices and our behavior and we decide anew. We live through crises and disappointments and surprises and losses and we keep going. We grow and we experience depths we hadn't imagined. Life shocks us all and, still, we persist.

Understandably, with this growth and openness we change in ways we couldn't predict when we were 21 and new adults. We learn that Life is for expanding, not for just tolerating *what is* and always has been. No box holds us.

We learn that our intellects aren't in charge. No matter what we said when we were 21, Life has opened possibilities to us. And we want to explore them. Sometimes we feel compelled to follow the inexplicable tugs that won't let us be satisfied. We don't choose this restlessness but we must honor it.

Somehow we know that our discontent is sacred. It emerges from a depth we haven't known but we trust it. For if we don't, we're sure we'll lose our soul. And that would be the greatest crime we could commit—foreclosing on our chance to be the individual we were born to be.

We watch and we notice and we observe Life working with us to heal and to grow and to express. So, we do. We join in this divine dance and celebrate ourselves as we evolve. We are as surprised as everyone else. In some ways our Life is not our own but we wouldn't change anything. We've discovered magic by allowing. The magic lives in our center and we allow it to emerge by listening and attending to the tugs and honoring our divine discontent. It's the only way we grow into ourselves.

Source Is

We can't change Source. We can't piss It off so badly that It wants to punish us. Likewise, we can't impress It so much It will indulge us. Source is.

We are becoming. We grow through having experiences. We touch fire and decide not to repeat that experience. We pet a cat and choose to do it again. We act, we decide, we choose. That's how we grow up. And along the way we make mistakes except that they are not mistakes. We are just learning and growing, doing our own experiments in becoming a human. What else can we do?

At the very core of who we are, Source is. We pursue different avenues which lead us into all sorts of experiences, some comfortable, some painful, but we learn from each. We may choose the academic route and earn a doctorate but Source is at our center. Or we may choose drug addiction, but, again, Source is at our center. We may delve into criminality, still Source is our center. Whatever we do with the conscious choices we make, the undeniable, unchanging unconscious reality is that Source is our center.

And Source is pure love and unconditional acceptance. For the doctor and the drug addict and the criminal. It doesn't matter to Source. Source is always the same—loving and accepting. Not a love we can earn or lose. Source is and always says Yes to each one of us. Yes, try that avenue. Yes, dive into that arena. Yes and yes. Do what you will. And through our actions we learn and grow and we continue to choose.

We refine our particular talents and skills and we make our own particular contribution. Each life is to grow into one's self. And we can do that however we want. Whatever we choose is acceptable.

Every choice has consequences and we will pay the consequences. So we learn and we grow.

Getting stuck in self-recrimination or losing sight of the big picture can muddle our thinking. When we decide that what we've done is overwhelmingly reprehensible and that we can never forgive ourselves, we block Source. Source is an ongoing process. When we calcify into self-hate we step outside that process. Source doesn't love us less for what we have done.

How can we learn to look at ourselves the way Source looks at us? We must lose our proprietary attitude about our lives and allow. Do we think it serves Source for us to hate ourselves? Don't we close Source off by doing that? When we show up and say, "I am here," then we allow Source. We watch and we don't know what will happen, but we pay attention.

It's not our job to punish ourselves. Appropriate guilt is understandable. But there is more. After twenty years of guilt and self-hate, what does Source want from us? After all, Source needs us to do Its work on earth. If Source prefers ongoing suffering, so be it. But if not, we'd better pay attention to discern what is asked of us. We are not the judge and jury of ourselves or anyone else. We merely accept what Source delivers and say, "Thank you." Maybe this lifetime we didn't get the rich and famous contract. Maybe we're doing loser and degenerate. So be it. Next lifetime will be different. Our job is to show up and to be available to learn. We don't have to choose correctly or to be good or to be happy. We just say, "Yes, and what am I to learn from this experience?"

All is experience. It's easier to acknowledge that when things are comfortable and rewarding. The successful doctor may struggle with self-acceptance as the murderer does but she has props around her to support her. The challenge of the murderer is to truly forgive himself and to find self-worth in the minutes of his day. And to go on and not to be defined by his past behavior.

And might that not be a bigger challenge than most of us face with our normal middle-class lives? Contributing to society in obvious ways may prevent us from going to places inside us that the murderer must approach. For him to retire into depression and to give up on himself is to deny Source. In trying to go on and to live a decent life, isn't he accepting a mission of imposing proportions? Isn't he choosing to say "Yes" to himself when the rest of us say "No" to him? How many of us are satisfied with locking a murderer up and forgetting about him? And what do we do with the challenges in our own lives? Do we shy away from looking at the darkest corners inside ourselves? Are we satisfied to live a two dimensional life and to be nice?

For we could all be the murderer. There is no one among us who is so pure that we can denigrate another no matter how serious his offense. We each have it within ourselves to commit the blackest deeds. Circumstance may offer us a reprieve. But can we judge those who have lived a more intense life just because we fear our own intensity? Perhaps it is because we know that in some place in us, we are the same as the one we judge.

When we allow, we identify with the Source-consciousness that is our core. We see the Source-consciousness in everyone else. And we know that is the truth.

R2 L2

A simple spiritual prescription for a successful life: release resentment and let your light shine.

No problem, you may say. Great! I respond. So we agree: there's no need to remember the hurts from last week or last year or twenty years ago. No clinging to childhood fears which inhibit your Adult from acting maturely. No lingering depressions. You don't take the world personally. Nothing requires a reaction, right? Well . . . maybe . . .

Behind resentment lies intolerable vulnerability. If it were tolerable, we would have stayed present to our feelings and, thus, healed them. Because we couldn't tolerate the hurt or the shame or the sadness or the fear, we shielded our soft side with a tough protective layer of anger. We may have fled to our intellect, further distancing our hearts from our everyday life.

Then we're left not feeling so much pain but with a tendency to snap at insensitive folks who step on our virtual toes. We become impatient with those losers (everyone) who can't appreciate us. Little frustrations grow into major problems. Paranoia looms. You may be quick to dismiss your unease as "their" problem or just part of the human condition. But, if in your heart you're not comfortable trusting that who you are is valuable and wanted, if you feel tied up inside, if you don't express yourself uniquely and creatively, then maybe there is a block.

Healing is possible, no matter how old the wounds. Past life material? No problem; that can be relieved, also. We move into the Adult part of us and we find the Child who was there so many years ago when Dad was drunk (or distracted) and Mom was furious (or powerless). And we embrace that hurting Child who still lives within us. Now we can be the Good Parent. Better than anyone else, we know what that Child feels and wants and needs to hear. And in our strong and resilient Adult we can provide love and guidance and consolation for our Child. We can be the sensitive, committed strong Parent the Child can safely depend upon. Healing ensues from that alliance.

With healing, the Child matures. And the world looks different—not so threatening or evil. Because we responsibly attend to our inner world needs, we experience the outer world without projection. We have cleaned the scrim through which we see.

And from this standpoint we're free to express the light at our core. Wherever our passion lives, our challenge as healthy adults is to express, express, express. We move into our deepest center, breathe and be, listen, wait, and allow ourselves to be guided. We pay attention, we say "Yes" and we express. We draw or sing or act or dance or compose but our personal source shades the inspiration which flows through us.

Squelching our creative voice cripples us and deprives the world of our unique contribution. We respect our artistic consciousness for we are all artists with our consciousness. We cannot afford to be nice or to say the appropriate and expected words or to leave ourselves open to be drained. Our loyalty sides with the light at our creative core. Fiercely we protect and nurture that light and we never apologize for being ourselves. We live passionately and deeply. And that's embracing our spiritual nature.

The Greatest Prayer

Some say our greatest prayer is "Thank you." It's a prayer available to us when we are overwhelmed. It's a prayer we can choose when we feel hopeless. It's a prayer which thrusts us from a perceived position of victim to one of partner.

Saying "Thank you" empowers us. We actively choose to engage in the current situation knowing that Source works beneath the surface. We willingly cooperate although we can't say how or with what. We simply declare, "I am available and I trust." And then we pay attention.

We always know that we are protected. We prefer to move to the level of solution rather than wallow at the level of problem. Power lies in that choice and we own our power when we say, "Thank you."

Choosing to align with the flow in the Universe reflects our awareness of our oneness. Always we are one but when we say "Thank you" we acknowledge it consciously. We release our struggle and any resentment or frustration. We relax and exhale and let it be.

"Thank you. For *whatever is* right now, thank you."

Our Two Challenges

Self-awareness is our first life challenge and self-acceptance is our second. First we struggle with the inner conflicts inherent in being human—Am I good enough? Do I do enough? Am I worthy?

These questions exert an unconscious pull on our daily energy. Our doubts and fears are real and demand our attention. So we do our healing work in the first decades of our lives. We work through layers of self-condemnation, shame, and hurt—over and over—until we sincerely arrive at a place of peace. That peace at our center can't be shaken or diminished after we have acknowledged every critical thought and heartache.

Genuine self-acceptance emerges only then. Self-acceptance is not pride. I don't accept myself because I'm proud of what I've accomplished. I don't accept myself for any "good reason." Self-acceptance isn't based upon performance.

After I have worked through conflicts and healed wounds in the first half of life, I move to a level in myself deeper than my mind can access on its own. In meditation I experience my divinity and I carry that "knowing" that truly lives in me wherever I go. The peace and self-acceptance that results shifts my awareness from a purely personal viewpoint to a transpersonal stance. I don't have to react to anything. I know that at my core I am better than I am at my personality-constricted moments.

Once I have experienced Source's acceptance of me, not for what I've done but just for being, I can accept myself. And since I can accept myself, I can accept others. In fact, I have learned to greatly respect the men I have known through my work in prison. Some of those who have committed murder and served twenty to thirty years for their crime have spent their lives searching their souls.

First, they reach sobriety which often takes two to five years. (Addictions to alcohol and drugs influence 95% of the crimes committed in the state penitentiary where I work.) Most of these men were young, rebellious, and impulsive. They chose experiences over safety and pushed aside fear. They took whatever consequences ensued from their unlawful behavior, saying, "I took a risk. I knew what might happen."

And they have lived in cramped, inhuman conditions, not complaining. After so much time they say, "It doesn't matter where my body is. I pray and I meditate and I am available to my comrades. What more is there?" And they smile slightly and turn away.

I can feel their peace. They don't struggle or resist or judge. They have moved past the self-hate which dominated their consciousness for more than a decade after they became sober. Upon realizing the gravity of their actions and the pain they have created for their victim's family and for their own family, they have forgiven themselves. One man said to me, "I could spend my life despising myself as I did for fifteen years or I can get on with it and be of service to someone else."

Learning self-acceptance in these circumstances can instruct us all. I view these men as advanced spiritual students who went to the lowest points a human can reach. They were willing to experience themselves as vile, horrid, worthless beings condemned by respectable folks.

And then they committed to stay on their own side and eventually brought themselves out of their misery. They suffered for decades moving deeper inside. Comfort was never a possibility for them. Distractions were non-existent. Their lives have been focused on survival in soul terms. Not one of them set out consciously to pursue spiritual development but when there was nothing else, they moved in the only direction they could—inward. Because they had no hope of escape, they kept their focus on their centers. After years they came to their own place of peace and forgiveness and self-acceptance.

What a journey they undertook.

At the Level of Peace

When you don't like what you see, you're offered the opportunity to see beyond the level of challenge to the level of peace. In other words, *what is* isn't the problem; it's how you see it. The good news is that you can change the way you see in one second. Always, no matter *what is* you have the choice of saying "Yes." You can drop your resistance to anything at will. And when you drop your resistance, there isn't a problem!

When you operate at the level of peace, there are no problems, only opportunities. "What am I offered the opportunity to learn from this situation?" Never is blaming and self-righteous withdrawal the answer. In an instance where you are Obviously Right, you're being given the chance to see deeper. What is going on? "I'm Obviously Right and yet they don't see it and don't acknowledge me and it pisses me off!" Maybe you need to look at your anger. It's always a gift when our hidden dynamics are illuminated.

When you operate at the level of peace you say, "Thank you." No matter *what is*, no matter how you feel about it, you say, "Thank you." You don't judge, you don't resist, you don't criticize. "Thank you."

Humbling, isn't it? You can never Be Right. You can't look down your nose at that poor misguided bloke who is so different from you. You can't spar and humiliate or gossip and denigrate. You are simply here. You accept *what is* and you say "Thank you."

At the level of peace you are asked to let go. You don't hold onto resentment. You don't relive anything from more than two minutes ago. You don't over-think. Discontent is a sign that you're being invited to express more of your soul consciousness. So, you gladly embrace your discontent and open to whatever comes.

At the level of peace, you surrender and you trust. You know when you are responsible and you know what's not in your control. You don't let details mire you down. Always you keep an eye on the Big Picture—your inevitable growth and development. You know you are being guided and you expect gifts.

Our Essence

The inmates at the state penitentiary where I work often get stuck in their self-hate. They committed an awful crime with severe consequences for others. They have made bad and worse choices for years. And they have alienated their families who supported them as long as they could. They are hated by many and have learned to hate themselves.

Most of us who are not incarcerated shield ourselves with titles and achievements. We learn to develop an imposing façade. The inmates can't do that. We listen to our Controller and it says, "Keep going. Don't stop." And we pretend that we feel good about ourselves. The inmates listen to their Controller and it says, "You messed up big time and you don't deserve a break." The process is the same—we move away from our center into the Controller in our heads to convince ourselves we're OK. Or, in the case of the inmates, not OK.

The inmates forget they are more than what they did. Behavior is one thing and something for which we are responsible. But the core of our being is something else. The essence of who we are is Source. It's easy to forget that for all of us. That's why we go back to that stillness at our deepest center each day and we stop and we pay attention.

And when we pay attention, we never hear from our Controller, not in our center. The Controller voice is from our heads. In our center, we are never judged and condemned and forgotten. Source always says Yes to us. We cannot alienate ourselves from Source or hide from Source or fool Source.

We do face enormous challenges and we do have lessons to learn and we must reconsider our thinking. But our essence is Source. In each second, if we stop and pay attention inside we encounter Source. And that's really all we have to do—be present and experience.

"Be still and know that I am God" is not as easy as it sounds. Knowing that each of us is Source is a burden as well as a joy. Everything counts—every utterance, every thought, every decision, every action. Source is everywhere we are. There are no time outs.

So, of course, we can't tolerate self-hate. That blocks us from our experience of Source at our core. Somehow we have to be present to Source's acceptance, Source's "yes," and balance our responsibilities in the world. No matter what we've done, we don't forego our responsibility to be present to the rest of our lives. We always have another second and another decision and another opportunity. And we don't want to miss those by getting stuck in the past.

Forgiveness is saying today is as important as yesterday. However I lived yesterday I can make another choice today. I can always go on. And wherever I am, Source is.

Allowing Healing

We allow healing. We can't will it or force it or buy it. Consciousness is the basis for healing. We can maintain an attitude of openness and humility, paying attention to the details of our experience. And we can say, "I am available."

Our thinking is a major component of healing but healing isn't primarily intellectual. All of us have distortions in our perception and our processing of information. We see outside what we don't want to see inside. We block feelings without consciously knowing we do so. Our thinking wants to keep us comfortable, not vulnerable.

Yet, vulnerability is essential. No matter if the healing is physical or emotional or spiritual, it's all one. Each of us is one person with different aspects. When we focus on the particular dysfunction in one aspect of us we lose sight of the whole—the complete individual whose eternal core is consciousness.

That core is where healing happens. What isn't integrated needs healing. What we don't like needs healing. Anything less than powerful requires healing.

Integration, peace, and power come from our perfect core. They already exist in us this second. We need to discard the distracting overlays that tell us we are not good enough. And that requires psychological work to heal the wounds that gave rise to that belief.

Before we feel our old pain and release it, we notice friction in our encounters with others. Any distortion in our beliefs about ourselves will be magnified by our interactions. Then we move inside and allow healing.

Healing happens when we feel our feelings, look at our beliefs, and keep breathing. Healing demands that we tolerate our uncomfortableness and look at it with detachment. We breathe, we feel, we notice, and we keep breathing. We watch the healing move through us when we step aside and observe. We move into our vulnerability and allow and stay present and focused every second.

And then we do it again, every day. We learn to trust the healing process and to follow its lead. We attune ourselves to receptivity. We, thereby, learn surrender. And with surrender we heal.

What's Source Got To Do With It?

Sometimes I hear it said, "How could God let that happen?" I always laugh to myself. Isn't that like us humans to not take responsibility for what we have done? The world is exactly as we have made it. Are we horrified? Yes. Rightfully so. Do we change? Not appreciably.

After the tragedy of 9/11 we were urged to return to normalcy. Shouldn't that event have shaken us so dramatically that we reflect upon our lives, how we have lived, and how we want to live? Wasn't that a wake-up call of overwhelming proportions? Why would we want to return to our 9/10 way of living? Weren't we given a glimpse that something we're doing on earth isn't working?

Why are we so afraid of looking deeply into ourselves? We feel such resistance to just experiencing consciously *what is*. I suspect we are all caught in fear and we can't find our way out. Humans are such terrified little beings. Rambo and Star Wars are just a fancy front for a trembling infant. I meet people who will engage in cut throat negotiations but won't stop for a few minutes just to breathe and to feel what it is to be themselves that moment. Are our inner worlds that dangerous?

I know they are not but I also know the depth and intensity of the pain that lies hidden there. Feeling that is nothing to brush off lightly. But we get through it and it passes and we are more whole for the journey. What do we think this life is for anyway? This isn't IT. We're just preparing. Working out the kinks. Developing some grace, perhaps, in our attention. Learning to let go of attachment and fear. Realizing what is important.

And what is that? After we reach 50, many of us gain a perspective that ambition and self reliance had previously clouded. The new perspective extends inside ourselves into our depths and behind our fears and we can accept increasingly more of ourselves, warts and all.

I think that's what Source is going for. Not simply a pleasant environment on earth. Not an easy status quo. But radical self acceptance. And that hurts! We can't fool Source and after 50 it's time to stop fooling ourselves.

Response And Response-Ability

So much of spiritual attunement is being available. Attunement implies a sensitive attention and readiness. A spiritually attuned life is not one that is planned in advance. It is not one that knows the answers or even the questions. Attunement is a process, a way of being. If the "doing" aspect becomes too important, attunement is lost. Whether it is doing good works or doing evil deeds or just doing the list of chores the job demands, it is the attitude and the attunement that count. With whom/what is the primary relationship? Is it with the demanding Controller who is most interested in checking off the to-do list? Or is it with the spontaneous daily flow of Life? What are we responding to? Where is our attention directed?

I find that I am easily seduced by my Controller. It is hard for me to believe that Source would be satisfied with my working 1-2 hours a day and watching television in the evenings. Certainly, my Controller doesn't condone that schedule. Not enough suffering or struggle. Source does not require struggle. Actually, the fastest route to Source is to release all struggle, not to have a position, and to accept *what is*. A simple "Thank you" suffices.

Why is that so hard for us humans?

My theory is that it is not because we would have to admit that we are not Source and accept a submissive position, but that we would have to admit that we are Source, that there is no difference between an all powerful Presence and the core of ourselves, and that, in fact, what is being asked of us is what we long for already–oneness. What a kettle of fish that is! We act like we are gods and that we want to work our wills and now we hear Source saying, OK, You are. Do what you want.

I don't know about you but that leaves me sputtering. Immediately my Controller intrudes and wants to structure the experience for me—Be perfect. Think before you speak. Be careful! And I stop breathing and become completely self-conscious. I think I can hear giggling in the background.

Accepting our oneness is another letting go, not taking on a new burden. It is not about performance that comes from a belief in separateness but from doing less. Doing as little as possible, actually. Waiting for direction and then acting instead of choreographing our weeks and months. It is not about having a five year plan.

What is this, you say? I am an adult. Any baby can do nothing. I have more to offer than that.

Do you? Unfortunately, Source may not be interested. It wants an open heart and an open mind. Do you have that to offer? Are you available to feel any feeling that arises in you without reacting? Are you open to reconsidering your strongly held political beliefs? Would you take that person who irritates you so much to lunch? About that one whom you criticize in your mind, can you say he and I are one? He shows me myself? Where is the line that is hard for you to cross? At Jesse Helms? Or Jesse Jackson? You are one with each of them.

On the surface the pre- and the trans- of spirituality have some commonalities—humility, spontaneous accepted feelings, presence in the moment. But a mature spirituality is based in a state that has developed a strong sense of individuality and then moved beyond it. So much transformational writing discusses the ego in pejorative terms, but having a strong ego is essential to the development of a mature spirituality. It is not a virtue to retain one's innocence past the time when one has been called to be powerful. Innocence is a given. Living adds experience. Refusing experience is refusing to grow into one's power. Individual power is a maturing and a refinement of the being we are born with. Trying to maintain the purity of a neonate is refusing Source.

Life demands that we engage. Participating in life soils us. We make mistakes and we cause pain. We acknowledge our responsibility and clean up our behavior. We do our work in therapy and clean out our closets packed with repressed material from our pasts. Each of these steps is essential but not sufficient for a mature spirituality. Responsibility extends to correct behavior, to emotional healing of our inner wounds, and then to the availability to respond to Source in the moment.

We become increasingly more passive as we learn what living responsively/responsibly entails. Our action is directed and chosen, not compulsive to avoid our fears. We operate from a peaceful reserve which is funded by our daily practices of experiencing oneness (meditation, yoga, visualization, affirmations, prayer, journal writing). We are present to the moment and fully alive. We don't struggle. Whatever happens we accept and say, "Thank you," and we breathe.

That's all.

Our Three Judges

We're given trials as part of our life journey. An expected good doesn't materialize. A friendship ends badly. We lose what we thought we'd gained. Surprise disappointments dot our days. What do we do?

For each trial we're assigned three judges. Our inner Critic has been with us seemingly forever. Characteristically, he responds, "It's your fault. Just another example of how you are not good enough." We sigh and hurt and feel ashamed. That's his job—to shame us and hurt us and leave us further away from our Adult.

The second judge is the Observer we practice when we meditate. The Observer is grounded, has no agenda, and is present to *what is* at each second. The Observer notices . . . and releases . . . and notices . . . and releases. No matter *what is* the Observer remains detached, never condemning or belittling, just acknowledging.

The third judge is the divine I Am. This judge knows that your core is good and deserving of good. Your behavior doesn't affect this judge's total unconditional acceptance. Whatever you did in the past is unimportant to this judge for It focuses on the present and the future. It knows you have another choice and another chance today and tonight and tomorrow.

Its concern is very long term. It will support you in learning what you need to learn and It doesn't limit you or pressure you. You may have all the experiences you want. It doesn't condemn you for your choices or love you less but It does insist that you grow.

The first judge has the loudest voice and the most familiar one. The second judge allows us to look at the first judge without being destroyed. The third judge opens our hearts and allows us to believe in ourselves. Because It knows that we deserve the highest and the best, we can know it, also. We can learn to listen to this judge and to see the world as It sees it and to see ourselves with Its gentleness and compassion and trust. Lovingly, It invites us to grow into ourselves.

Keeping Source Small

We limit Source. We want to understand Source in terms that are familiar. We prefer to think of Source as an indulgent grandparent or a withholding administrator. We want to make Source into something we know. That way this whole Source thing becomes handle-able.

But the truth is Source isn't handle-able, we can't manage Source, and we can't possibly comprehend the power and extent of Source. We can experience Source in our own particular terms but beyond that we're intellectualizing. And that's a sure way to distance ourselves from Source. With our minds in the picture, there isn't room for Source.

Source is an experience and that experience is momentary. It's immature to say that Source wants you to be good. For heaven's sake, that was your mother! You're not a child any longer. Grow up and open to Source in grown-up terms. No more self-indulgence, no more hope of being saved from yourself, no more innocence. It's inappropriate to pretend guilelessness if you're over fourteen.

Source offers engagement and redirection and reflection and change. Source is not an authority who can be manipulated. Source is and Source lives in your every cell. Source is not out there, you can't avoid being known by Source, and you can't wrestle anything from Source. It's all yours right now and always has been and always will be. Source is a state of being to experience.

If it's so simple, why don't we all just open to Source and say, "Here I am" and relax? My theory is that we don't really want to know Source. We don't want to experience our oneness with Source and we don't want to lose our boundaries. We'd rather be separate and think we're in control of our lives than surrender. Then maybe, we think, we can be somebody.

By midlife we've gone lots of places and tried lots of things. We know the outside world pretty well. We're established in business and in our lives and we think we know who we are. Life has been predictable and relatively logical until midlife. Then slowly the bottom falls out and the rules change and we realize we don't know who we are at all. And that's when we can open to know Source. It's our choice. If control is still a big word for you, surrender might terrify. We have had many many opportunities to learn that we are not really in control. Nevertheless, our minds still try to convince us that we can yet work our own will if we only persevere. We can live out our lives in that vein if we choose. We can forego mystery and magic and adventure because our Controller doesn't want those experiences anyway.

If, however, we've had enough pain and we've cried enough tears and we can't do the same old thing in the same old way one more time, well, then we open and say, "I am available." Partly it's out of exasperation. We've seen repeatedly that our will can only do life in its most mundane aspects. And partly it's out of excitement—we want the magic and the mystery that beckon and we'd hate to die having foreclosed on those options.

And that's when we're ready to know Source. We stop. We move inside. We wait. We say, "Yes" to what we don't know, but we know we're available. And then we accept whatever happens.

Source's Playground

The mundane world is the playground for Source. It plays "gotcha" with us. When we lose our cool and growl at our neighbor— "Gotcha!" When we blame someone for anything at all—"Gotcha!" When we take offense, personalizing another's remark—"Gotcha!" We step out of our center, we forget to accept everything that comes, we resent anything at all, and the gotcha's vibrate in the air.

Being right is not a choice. There is no right or wrong, just *what is*. No rules apply. It's not about domination. We're not competing to prove our worth. We are. We can open to having experiences or we can close our hearts and lick our wounds and pity ourselves. If we choose, we can hold our heads up, encounter the day with humility, and say, "Thank you." No matter what comes, "Thank you."

We are the perpetual student, never the Judge. We learn from everything. When another "in authority" disrespects us we say, "Thank you." What is "fair" is not a consideration. What "I deserve" is irrelevant. We learn humility and self-respect by saying "Thank you" and by practicing forgiveness. We don't need to wrest justice from the world. We need to stay centered, keep our hearts open, practice forgiveness and love, and be present to each moment.

If not many others practice this discipline, that's OK; it's their choice. We are not treated as we would like. So we learn to forgive and to see into their perfect center and to bless them. We have the experiences we need, not the ones we find comforting. Circumstances don't matter; what we learn from our experience counts. The outer world fades soon enough. It's the inner world that goes on and on. Our home lies within us, in our deepest center. In our essence we allow our true self to be and to grow and to evolve. That's all that is important.

Experiencing Source

A spiritual experience is one in which we experience Source. Source is. When we pay attention we notice. It doesn't matter what we see or where. It's the quality of our attention that lends sacredness to the moment.

When I walk into the men's penitentiary where I work, I experience Source. I'm aware of suffering. I sense despair. I feel Source in the air. The custody officers are solemn, the inmates withdrawn (or maybe abusive). But I recognize the immediacy and the urgency and the power of each moment. And I know that's Source.

Where humans ache, Source lives. When we wonder if we will survive, Source abides. In our confusion and misery and hopelessness, Source waits.

I see Source in the inmates when they talk about cleaning their 6 x 9 foot cells which they share with another man. I hear Source when the inmates speak about their struggles with drugs—they know they shouldn't touch them but they don't know if they can resist. I feel Source when the lifers offer a pleasant thought–I know that they choose acceptance. Source is present in the moments when these men question what it means to live a meaningful life.

The lifers especially must delve within themselves to find a way to survive. They are faced with the possibility of never walking 100 yards in a straight line ever again. Maybe they will never crack an egg or wear their own clothes. And yet they find purpose in Hospice when they sit with their fellows who are dying. In the evenings they teach younger inmates to read in the Literacy program.

One said to me last week that he expects to be released soon (after 25 years) but if not, that's OK. He has learned that his inner world peace is all that counts; it doesn't matter where his body is. And I experienced Source in that moment.

A Mature Spirituality

Being in partnership with Source as co-creators of our lives is active as well as passive and receptive. But it is active in the details, not the overall picture. We ask for the highest and the best for our lives, we repeat, "I allow," and we focus on the steps we take today. In our partnerships we don't see the path. We allow the path to present itself to us.

So, our activity follows our passivity and is directed by what we receive in our hearts, not from the constructs of our minds. Our activity is like the two-year-old who toddles away from mom, looks back, touches her knee, and then explores the room again. We are always checking in with Source. Have we lost our centers? Are we coming from our hearts? We monitor the temper and tone of our action. When we feel solid, we move.

Maturity is not struggling. It involves waiting and accepting our place humbly and following as we are led. It also involves joy and excitement and energy. But we don't create that. We are available and we receive. Addiction is our effort to create what we know is missing instead of feeling its absence and allowing our wounds to heal. Love addiction tries to create the oneness with another human that by rights belongs to our relationship with Source. Food addiction tries to erase the gaping hole we feel inside when we sense our lack of wholeness. Substance abuse seeks to approximate the well being which is only solidly rooted in a mature spirituality. All of these addictions are attempts to procure the result (oneness) without doing the healing work that is ours to do as humans on this earth.

Immaturity is trying to find satisfaction in something other than Source. We know we are not complete but we prefer to use our heads and our backs to find comfort instead of surrendering to the wisdom of our inner worlds to heal us. We like to rely on our minds but our minds are always looking for a solution instead of trusting the process that is healing and wholing for us.

Maturity knows when to wait and when to act. Maturity is always connected. Maturity doesn't look for solutions but knows that commitment to the life process is the answer. Maturity is what Source asks of us. Not obedience, not self denial, not arrogance, not success. Simple maturity.

A mature spirituality is the only basis for partnership. How can we partner with Source if we are still identified with the Needy Child or the Driven Executive? How can we even see Source if our vision is blocked by identification with an unhealed part of ourselves? Maturity is based on our allowing ourselves to be healed, not trying to make ourselves OK by our actions. For it is in that healing process that we partner with Source. We cannot heal ourselves. It requires maturity to acknowledge that limitation and courage to allow Source to work in us.

Oneness

Most of the inmates at the state penitentiary where I work were drug addicts—heroin, marijuana, cocaine, LSD, whatever they could get. They speak about chasing their first high, always remembering a more intense experience than they've had since and not being able to recreate it. They didn't abandon the chase until incarceration forced the end.

In the meditation groups I ask if our meditations are similar in any way to their drug highs. The long time meditators say, "Yes, but without coming down." Longing for the experience of oneness may be the soul of drug addiction. And isn't that the core human drive? We seek love, friendship, or success but these diversions so often leave us dissatisfied. We achieve what we say we want and within minutes we want something more. Why?

My suspicion is that on a cellular level we know we are missing something we need to be whole. On an intellectual level we can't identify what that is but we substitute "definable" solutions. We long for peace inside but we focus on making money. That's something we can control. Who can force peace? We want happiness which we can't make happen on cue so we enjoy chocolate which we can buy any time. The inmates used drugs. What's the difference? Control of something finite substitutes for oneness with the Infinite. For a minute.

I don't know of one person who would say that what s/he seeks in life more than anything else is oneness with Source but I suspect that that is the human condition. We somehow know that there is more to existence than meets the eye. We can't place it so we try to structure an experience that we can define. We must redefine Source in limited terms so our minds can be involved in the act. Better to use our minds than to allow unlimited vulnerability.

But "allowing" and "vulnerability" are what knowing Source is about. We imprison Source when we say, "This (read: money, love, power) will make me happy." When we try to define Source, we limit Source. When we want to assume an overlay of happiness without doing our undercover work, we shy away from Source. We hate not being in control and when we are in control, we imprison Source. We want Source not to threaten us. We want Source to fit into our lives neatly. We want Source to keep us comfortable.

When comfort is necessary, Source gets squeezed out. Unlimited power cannot be controlled or fit into our little boxes and it doesn't come on schedule on Sunday morning. We don't dictate terms to Source about what we will or won't accept. We say, "I am available" and we watch. When we surrender our lives, we don't know what will happen. And if you need to be in control, surrender is not a "reasonable" choice.

So, if we accept the premise that experiencing oneness with Source is the basic human longing and if we acknowledge that losing our boundaries terrifies us humans, then we find ourselves in a pickle of gigantic proportions. For a few years or decades we look for Source under the street light, so to speak. We want Source in small doses, easily digested. We're satisfied with our Source-in-a-box. And that's the end of the story for many many folks.

Some of us won't let go of the search that easily, however, and by mid-life we won't engage in illegal activity or reckless risk-taking. What are we to do? We need to experience our oneness with Source because without that we're lost. Nothing else holds meaning.

The vastness of our inner world and the pervasiveness of our life experience when we surrender and trust in meditation and then throughout the day leads us to experience Source minute by minute. And then we don't want to stop. Even when it's scary or unpleasant or inconvenient. And I think that's what the drug addicted inmates sought in their own unsavory way. They are just being humans. On some level they knew there is more. They detoured with drugs but find some peace in meditation. They are acting like human beings.

Presence

Owning our power is the opposite of how it sounds. It isn't about increasing anything but about letting go. Letting go of the defenses we have unconsciously assumed to get us through life whether that be working hard or avoiding work. Whatever we chose which reduced our anxiety and told us how to proceed, well, now at midlife we release that. If our Controller told us to be good, now we step back and look at that Controller. So many of the new meditators I meet in the meditation group talk about what they've read and how they imitate that.

I like to use meditation as an example of how we live life. Meditation is just being present to the moment. We don't know what we will experience. We just show up and say "I'm available." When a new meditator comes to group talking about the latest Wayne Dyer PBS show, I know we have some adjusting to do. I love Wayne Dyer and I watch the PBS installments eagerly. However, at meditation time I want to focus on being present to *what is* inside me at that second. As long as we stay in our heads looking outward at another, we cannot be present in meditation.

Meditation is life cut small. Whatever we do in meditation we do in life but probably without awareness. In meditation we turn on the spotlight and simply notice *what is.* If we power our way through life using our minds, that's what we will see in meditation and that's great. As long as we don't identify with our minds. Or maybe it's not your mind that provided you with a vehicle to motor through the exigencies of the first half of life. Maybe it was your humor or your athletic ability or your appearance or your charisma. Whatever we chose (long ago when we didn't know we were choosing it) to ease our way has curtailed our aliveness. Whatever we have done, we look at in meditation. We notice the process which by now seems natural.

Folks who identify with their Controller do what they do to be right or good or appropriate. But we don't meditate for any of those reasons. We meditate to be. We just "be" and notice what it is "to be" this second. Fairly simple but what consternation it arouses! Meditation provides us with a snapshot of how we live. And it's how we live that's the backdrop for owning our power. So meditation helps us see *what is*.

The magic part of mid-life (and meditation) is the power of the unconscious to heal. Suddenly (it seems) something inside us brings us to experiences which release any tension we've maintained. And if we've lived listening to our Controllers we've probably stored a lot of tension over the years. So we meditate which is to say to Life, "I'm available to be healed. I don't need to hold onto the shield my Controller has provided. I'm ready to see Life for what it is. More importantly I'm ready to experience Life without padding to reduce its shock." In meditation we say "Yes, I'm available this second. And this second. And this second." And that is what owning our power is about.

Meditation certainly isn't the only way to effect this shift. It's just an easy way to notice it. Owning our power comes down to not using our defenses, not structuring our experience, not closing off parts of ourselves, just being present to receive. Because when we get out of the way, we notice that Life has its own guidance for us and it's not what our minds have concocted. Owning our power is saying "Yes" to Life. Not "Yes, I think that's a good idea so I'll try it for a day." Owning our power is assuming a totally different relationship to Life.

In mid-life we move an additional step and say, "My primary relationship is with my inner world and I will trust its guidance no matter what. I won't put stipulations on the guidance I receive.

I won't say, Now remember, Life, I don't want to be homeless and I don't want to be uncomfortable and please make sure retirement is pleasant." No. Owning our power is a complete letting go. It's saying, "Yes, I am available." And saying that again every day.

Prosperity

We're all in favor of prosperity. We think it means accumulating possessions, buying anything we want, doing what we prefer, going where we choose. But that's not prosperity; that's indulgence— immature and irresponsible. Prosperity is aligning our consciousness with the flow that already exists.

Consciousness refers to aliveness in tiny bits, the "is-ness" of life. It's not what we think; it's how we "be." How available are we to ourselves? Are we present to *what is* inside us at any given second? Through our experience—what we learn and infer from what happens to us and what we do—we unknowingly shape our consciousness.

After some life experience and with some awareness of our consciousness, we acknowledge "flow." Flow describes natural movement in universal consciousness. Our minds don't manufacture flow. No human created flow. Flow is. Our participation in the flow reflects our consciousness, specifically, our availability.

As with any kind of abundance, money flows. We receive and we give. If we hoard, we stop the flow. If we're closed to receiving, we stop the flow. If our hearts are open, we trust the flow. We allow wealth/love/abundance to come to us. And we share our wealth/love/abundance. We participate in the flow which is larger than we are.

In addition to receiving, we release. Traditionally, tithing at church or to the source of our inspiration serves this purpose. But releasing money for a cherished piece of art or to help a friend or even to pay a gambling loss supports our letting go. We never grumble; we always express gratitude that we can share our wealth. Releasing joyfully is as important as receiving.

Releasing facilitates receiving. If you want money to come to you, practice releasing in advance. That creates a void which must be filled. Money operates by the law of flow. If you feel stuck and you can't seem to force abundance to come to you, practice giving joyfully. Do volunteer work. Offer your services to someone who needs them. Empower the flow by participating as you can—by giving in any way. If you release with an open heart and an open mind, you will receive what you need.

And when money comes, allow it to flow through you and to keep moving. It's not yours to grab. You need not fear. The flow doesn't stop. We immerse ourselves in it and trust it and enjoy it. And that's true prosperity.

When we know our place in the universal flow and we trust surely and without question, we are wealthy. We don't fear, we don't connive, we don't over-think, and we don't worry. We are present and available, we appreciate *what is* this minute, and we give thanks. Only then do we experience true prosperity.

Availability

Knowing reality involves more than opening our eyes and looking around. "Seeing" happens when we are ready to see. Seeing depends upon our availability. It's not similar to plunking ourselves down in front of a TV and passively acknowledging movement around us. Seeing roots in our soul.

What does "availability" mean?

Availability refers to showing up and being present without a thought to the impression we make or to the feelings which arise inside us. We're not paying attention to other people or to circumstances. All our focus and all our attention move inside. We say "I am available" and we wait and we pay attention. We don't know what thoughts, feelings, memories, insights will arise. We practice availability when we allow ourselves to go to any depth inside. We allow ourselves to be carried. When we practice availability we don't think or resist. We may notice our fear. In fact, we notice everything. But we commit to the ride. Wherever we are carried we practice presence.

Availability implies trust. We know that Source in us pulls us to healing in our own personal terms. We don't have to understand. We just show up and practice availability. Availability equals presence plus trust plus commitment with a healthy dose of humility. When we practice availability we defer to the highest and wisest part of us. We move into our own Source consciousness and we say "Yes. Yes, I am available. Yes, I commit to this ride. Yes, I accept guidance my mind can't fathom. Yes, I participate in my life but I don't own it. I allow life to teach me. I am available to learn. I acknowledge the Source within me. Yes to this second."

Loveable, Loving, Learning

We all yearn to be loved but traditional religion has taught us that we must work to be worthy of love. Being just as we are isn't good enough; there is something basically evil lurking in our shadowy innards. We don't know exactly what we lack but some authority will tell us and then show us how to correct our faults.

We listen, we try, but we never reach "good enough." In fact, we learn self-hate. We judge our feelings, alienate ourselves from our core, and live from our intellect instead of from our soul. We try to be other than how we are naturally and hope that that is more acceptable. To whom? To Source? To our mothers? To our peers (whom we fear only tolerate us)?

It certainly doesn't work with ourselves. We don't feel more comfortable. We don't like ourselves more. We don't experience increased aliveness and creativity and spontaneity and joy. We felt hurt and now we have layered pretense over the hurt. We're not aware of the hurt but it still lives in us. We know something is going on because we don't always sleep well and once in a while we drink a little too much and our eating seems designed to comfort our hearts instead of nourish our bodies. Generally, we're frustrated. This life doesn't seem worth it.

Can you imagine loving yourself the way you love a newborn— without expectation or criticism, with complete acceptance and open-hearted joy? With the trust that at your deepest core you are perfect? The truth is we are one with Source. That's the bottom line. Our foundation is Source; we cannot destroy that. We may forget our essence when we listen to the intellect but we remember ourselves when we move into our depths in meditation.

As individual expressions of Source we are loveable. We don't need to earn love. We can't improve on Source. We are fine this second.

The next level is practicing love. We are loving beings, sharing our acceptance and gratitude with others. Because we accept ourselves, we open our hearts and welcome others. We treat them the way we treat ourselves. We choose to be loving because that best expresses who we are.

We are always learning. We do takes and re-takes and mistakes because that's what life requires. We can't learn and grow without exploring different choices. We always get feedback and we always have another chance. And always we accept ourselves. "For this minute I am in my right and perfect place."

We open our hearts and we open our minds and we are open to new experience. We allow Source to be Source in us. What an adventure!

Let There Be Peace on Earth and Let It Begin with Me

Most of us have experienced terrible loss or shock or injury at some time in our lives. Each incident carried an emotional charge. For a while we relived it, experiencing the pain/fear/distress over and over. With time—maybe months or years—the feelings fade. We remember what happened but we don't feel the same intensity of emotion.

Eventually, we separate the event from our feelings about it. How do we do this? What do we really want to let go of? We will always have our memory, but when we come from our Peacemaker subpersonality, we put the event in perspective. A Peacemaker doesn't whine, criticize, or ridicule. A Peacemaker doesn't indulge in self-pity. A Peacemaker asks, "What am I to learn?"

A Peacemaker remembers Divine Order. In Divine Order, we never lose. We may not receive what we want this minute. In fact, we may endure hardship and loneliness and alienation for quite awhile. But we know that we are on a journey. Our journey is longer or shorter depending upon our resistance. We can move through the process with trust or terror but we are always in process. We create imbalance when we resent. We don't always get our way, but it doesn't mean that disaster is imminent. We trust in the wisdom of Divine Order which our minds can't grasp. Life is the principle of eternal growth and evolution. Life brings us every experience we need to grow. The Peacemaker knows that no matter *what is* this moment, her challenge is to open to the experience that Life offers.

The Peacemaker doesn't hold onto appearances. What we fear or hate will present itself to us. Our responsibility as Peacemakers is to stay focused on what is behind the appearance. We each have something which frightens us and it comes in different forms. Maybe our boss is unreasonably demanding, apparently abusive. Maybe our co-worker doesn't come through, abandoning us. Maybe an acquaintance insults us and doesn't apologize, apparently humiliating us publicly.

Our job as Peacemaker is to see behind the appearance and to ask "What provides my anxiety right now?" By doing that, we remember that we are larger than the circumstance. We don't get caught up in details—"He shouldn't have." "She wasn't fair." "That wasn't supposed to happen." The Peacemaker places each experience in the context of her life. And then learns from it.

Our affirmation of a truth we have not yet seen is our faith. We keep our faith in the Source of truth, not in the appearance. Accepting betrayal may offer us a doorway to a power we haven't imagined. Letting go of a cherished love may liberate our heart in an unexpected way. Accepting what we don't choose and don't like ushers us into a wider dimension of Life and allows Divine Order. The Peacemaker never refuses an experience. She says, "I allow Source to be Source in me and I watch. I allow Source to be Source in others and I watch. I allow Source."

Vulnerability, Fear, and Power

Mid-life brings an urgency to become ourselves—truly, wholly, authentically. What we have ignored inside ourselves now demands integration. For many of us that includes vulnerability. Just as sex was the dirty word of the Victorian age, vulnerability now is despised. It seems that people would rather tolerate abuse and rationalize that it really isn't abuse ("that's just the way she is") than to acknowledge that they are hurt by another's words. Feeling hurt is more feared than being physically injured. A football player will charge a line of oversized men but will not sit with his tears alone or in the company of his best friend. A business woman will work 14 hours a day without complaining or acknowledging her need for play. Anything to stay In Control.

Our years until mid-life have been devoted to augmenting our armamentarium of techniques to distinguish ourselves as valuable, desirable, and worthy. At mid-life, however, we must BE ourselves and that implies owning our unnoticed, despised, and unintegrated aspects. We realize that true power is not about dismissing what our minds fear but about owning the fear. We can't escape the traits we don't want to see and at mid-life we don't even want to escape because it's only ourselves we leave behind.

So we move into that vulnerability that has scared us so. We feel touched by a scene in a movie and we cry and then keep crying. We're offended by a mean-spirited comment and we don't pretend that we're not. How others see us isn't as important as being true to ourselves. Integrity becomes the overarching value. And with that commitment to our integrity, we allow ourselves to experience intense feelings when they come rather than trying to "understand" them.

Earlier in our lives sobbing for five hours alone on the floor would have terrified us. "What if I never stop crying?" we may have thought.

Holding onto Control for what seemed like our very survival was the first priority. All that has shifted now as living large compels us undeniably. So what if a tidal wave of emotion threatens to drown us? We've lived through our worst fears. We can live through whatever today brings, too. Suddenly, Control is not only irrelevant, it impedes our aliveness.

We invite today to bring its challenges. We want to face everything. We want to confront our fears. We want to experience what has scared us. And we know we can handle it, not because we have erected a giant ego but because we have learned the lesson and promise of surrender. We know that when we surrender to Life, we are carried through the storm to peaks we haven't before seen. We are shown vistas our eyes can't perceive when we hug the ground in avoidance of our feelings. Surrender carries us higher than we could manage by our own efforts.

We experience power that moves through us. We don't control it or even use it. We open to it and accept it and let it carry us. We realize that it isn't interpersonal. In fact, we feel humbled experiencing the roar of Life. And that's when we own our power—when we let Life happen and say "Thank you" no matter what. We have no enemies and no need to dominate or submit to another person. We see Life acting through others and realize we're all here to learn our lessons. Power is accepting our humble stance, speaking when spoken through, and knowing that staying in rapport with Source energy (as Wayne Dyer says) is our only job.

Only by moving deeply into our vulnerability and trusting it to carry us, do we realize what power truly is. We align with the Life force greater than our minds and subject our minds to it. When that force is clearly the one moving and directing us without input from our minds, we realize power. Paradoxically, power isn't about "doing" but about allowing. We allow Life to happen. We allow our reactions to occur and we don't act on them. We allow our feelings to arise and we accept them. We do less than we ever have and feel more ourselves–because we experience power moving through us, not coming from us. And that is the magic of mid-life—we grow into the fullness of our power through surrender and acceptance.

Gravitas is a word I especially like. It implies weight and dignity and knowing what you're about. A woman (or a man) with gravitas knows what's important. She's not thrown off her committed center path by wanting approval from anyone else. Losing pounds isn't more important than exercising her values. Speaking out against injustice is more valuable than fitting into an acceptable mold.

Many of us can act that part. Our behavior is beyond reproach, laudatory even. But the world isn't only what we can see and touch. Our inner world anchors gravitas.

Integrity contributes to gravitas. Being whole implies not ignoring our weakness and fear and hurt. Acknowledging every part of ourselves, regardless of what we would intellectually prefer were true, precedes integration. Perhaps we wish we weren't so quick to anger but the truth is that we are. And when we're angry we have to admit that we do things which aren't nice and which do hurt. And going even further, we realize that we don't mind if someone is hurt. In fact, we like feeling powerful enough to impact someone else.

But that isn't true power. Spreading pain isn't what we're about, no matter how justified we think it is. If we have to rationalize our actions or words, we know something doesn't fit. And if we have the intestinal fortitude to sit with ourselves, alone, in the darkest parts of our depths, we see that our own hurt underlies our hurtful words.

So, if we are committed to integrity and gravitas why don't we heal our own wounds? It seems like any adult would choose to do that.

When we commit to that healing path, however, we find that it takes us out of the adult realm and quickly deposits us into an irrational world with spooky characters and hungry quicksand and threatening monsters. And then what do we do?

Doing isn't of much relevance in the inner world. In there it's more about not doing. Not doing anything and feeling the fear which may be inherent in acknowledging vulnerability. Not doing and letting Life happen and waiting for a door to open or a word to be spoken by a stranger or a feeling we've been avoiding to arise. Not doing and choosing surrender to the healing process of our inner worlds.

When we work with Life from a position of surrender, then we open to true power. Then we don't come from our little egos in a defensive stance, ready to battle. When we move into the world undefended, not even knowing the answer but being willing to ask the question, then we embrace power.

We find that power isn't force. It isn't threats or selfish bragging or diplomas on the wall or money in the bank. Power isn't interpersonal. Power is basically an experience of unity within ourselves. We welcome everything that lives in us and we come to know it and integrate it. We make a commitment to our lives. We know that who we are and how we be matters. But we put the first step first. Healing ourselves.

Consciousness work (which healing ourselves is) offers our minute-to-minute experience meaning and depth. Consciousness is the "is-ness" of all being. We fracture that is-ness when we deny our vulnerability and pretend that we don't feel what we feel, when we act adult instead of holding the crying child within us, when we refuse to be present to our pain and our fear and our despair.

True power comes from integrating those parts of ourselves which are not what we like and not what we show to anyone and definitely not what we advertise. Seems paradoxical, doesn't it, that power implies not fighting vulnerability but owning it and embracing it and, thereby, integrating it. I agree that it's an uncomfortable process and one that any rational person would avoid if we could. But Life isn't about rationality and it's not about Control. Life isn't ours to mold (except in the details). The deep powerful flow is beyond any one of us but we all share in it. Relentlessly, we're carried to those places inside which are bruised, those hurts which are not healed, the spots where we haven't forgiven and, thus, can't move beyond. Our work this lifetime truly is about healing our consciousness. The integration of our consciousness with a consciousness greater than ours is another description of power. For by that integration we realize our place and we surrender and trust the Life flow. Power is that trust and that allowing and that basic surrender. We own our Power when we align with the Life force and say "I am available."

Peace

When I walked into church on Sunday, the small congregation was singing, "Peace will fill the world when we finally understand that only from within can it spread throughout the land." Peace isn't an external matter that can be legislated and enforced. Peace is a way of being—in harmony with ourselves, with others, and with the physical planet.

Peace starts inside. We contribute to world peace by healing our own poor self esteem, our fear, our old hurts, and by resolving our internal conflicts about accepting love. In that sense peace is a matter of being, not doing. It's not self indulgent to focus on the place inside that isn't still; it's our responsibility. Denial and looking good are not sufficient. No one else can heal us and what is inside of us is as much a part of the world as any other space.

Reality is far more than we can see and touch. The quantum physicists tell us that reality is not static and that we are not separate. The implications for our consciousness are huge. World peace is damaged when we belittle ourselves. It's not OK to diminish (or exaggerate) our value even in our own minds. We need to adopt the Golden Rule–treat ourselves as well as we treat others.

Personal empowerment implies respect for Life within us, realizing that we participate in a greater whole. We listen with detachment, acknowledging a wisdom we don't own. We allow it to guide us, acting from a peaceful center when we are called to do so. Global empowerment results from our respect for Life around us on the planet and in other people. Most of us will eagerly agree that we respect the planet and others and yet poverty, hunger, and disease continue. Why? Do we need another well-intentioned program or ten more or a thousand more?

Carl Jung told the story of a rainmaker visiting a village in Africa parched by drought for many months. He entered the tent prepared for him and stayed there alone for three days. On the fourth day rain fell. When asked what he had "done," he replied that he had picked up such imbalance when he walked through the village that he knew he must restore balance inside himself. When he did, balance was restored around him.

If each of us took responsibility for restoring balance inside ourselves, our planet would transform. We can't empower ourselves or our planet from our heads. We must commit our hearts to being present to anything unhealed within us and invite the healing that our minds can't fathom to work in us. When we live with that openness and that surrender to Life, healing will flood the planet.

When I left the church we sang, "Let there be peace on earth and let it begin with me." Each of us must commit to healing ourselves so that our planet can be healed. No one can do our work for us. Are you willing to do your part? The health of the planet depends on it.